# The 20 British Prime Ministers
# of the 20th century

*To my mother and in memory of my father —
the generation of 1945.*

# Attlee

DAVID HOWELL

HAUS PUBLISHING · LONDON

First published in Great Britain in 2006 by
Haus Publishing Limited
26 Cadogan Court
Draycott Avenue
London SW3 3BX

www.hauspublishing.co.uk

A CIP catalogue record for this book is available from the British Library

ISBN 1-904950-64-7

Designed by BrillDesign
Typeset in Garamond 3 by MacGuru Ltd
info@macguru.org.uk

Printed and bound by Graphicom, Vicenza

Front cover: John Holder

# Contents

# Part One

## THE LIFE

# Chapter 1: An Unlikely Socialist

The little man spoke to thousands in the cobbled marketplace. To his left, the spire of the parish church rose in the February dusk. He spoke in the clipped certainties of the educated military man. Here was traditional England. Yet this was Clem Attlee, Prime Minister of the first majority Labour government on the 1950 election campaign trail. He talked calmly of the government's record – no emotional appeals, no tricks of the orator. Somehow the absence of theatricality was impressive. He seemed strong. A young trade unionist, joining the crowd on his way home from work, would always recall that the little man was surprisingly tough.

Attlee's campaign had taken him to a place where traditional hierarchies of patronage and respect still mattered, where local notables bleated perpetually about the inequities of the socialist government. He responded with his vision of decency and togetherness. For the crowd, he was their Prime Minister. He answered their so-called betters, not as an outsider but as one born to security and privilege who had rejected capitalist values for a superior ethic. For just a few minutes, they saw Clem Attlee at his zenith, the respected leader of a government that had changed their world for the better. A week later they flocked to the polls in unprecedented numbers. They remembered how it had once been – and they had no wish to go back there.

Throughout those February days, Attlee, in his very ordinariness, represented the hopes of millions, yet he remained enigmatic. The middle-class, Oxford-educated gallant soldier who had discovered the working class in the Edwardian East End and converted to socialism, but who remained impeccably conservative in so much else, the dutiful party man who had somehow become party leader, the unexpected victor over Churchill in a post-war electoral earthquake – his life combined the unlikely and the unexpected.

Clement Richard Attlee was born into a socially stable and economically comfortable middle-class family on 3 January 1883. His birthplace, Putney, stood on the cusp between the village that it had been and the suburb that it was becoming. Affluent professional men commuted daily into the City of London. For Clement's father Henry, a partner in a firm of city solicitors, this daily journey structured his life. Industrious, reliable, predictable, the fruits of his labours were evident in the Putney house and later in an Essex country estate, and in the opportunities enjoyed by his eight children. If Henry epitomised the virtues of industry and integrity, his wife Ellen complemented such rigours with her enthusiasm for literature and the arts. The family were characterised by seriousness, sobriety and security. They were also happy and self-sufficient.

Religious observance was integral to family life. It was appropriately Anglican: the Attlee ethos did not suggest Nonconformist enthusiasm. The day began with prayers, both family and servants. Bible readings produced detailed knowledge of the New Testament. In later life Clement appeared sceptical, attributing this to the tedium of childhood Sunday services. Several siblings were not disenchanted. One brother Bernard was ordained; another, Tom, came to combine Christianity and socialism. A sister, Margaret, spent much of her life as a missionary and social worker in South Africa. An ethic of service influenced by an explicitly Christian commitment, or in Clement's case by a more secular morality, characterised this Attlee generation.

Attlee would later characterise himself as a Victorian. The London in which he grew up was very much the capital of Empire. Imperial trade flowed through the docks. The architecture of the West End increasingly spoke of imperial prestige. Queen Victoria's Golden and Diamond Jubilees, celebrated when Attlee was four and 14 respectively, were spectacular and self-congratulatory statements of global eminence and ambition. *Patriotism was the emotion of every free-thinking Briton.*[1]

Attlee's childhood was influenced by imperial pageantry and faith in the civilising mission of the humane British. But the 1880s were a decade of conflict and controversy. Irish land agitation was followed by a demand for Home Rule that divided the Liberal Party. In the same year, 1886, riots by the unemployed in the West End produced broken windows in fashionable clubs and much bourgeois paranoia. Three years later the London dock strike and the rise of an often militant 'new unionism' amongst those that the more respectable labelled as unskilled suggested, perhaps misleadingly, a radicalisation of the working class. Such events could seem far removed from privileged and protected Putney, apart from one socially embarrassing fact: Henry Attlee was a committed Liberal. William Gladstone was his icon. When Gladstone declared for Irish Home Rule, many middle-class supporters broke with the party, but Henry stuck by Liberalism. For the family, not

*In this country there was the established order. A class society was accepted ... The capitalist system was as unquestioned as the solar system. It was just there!*

ATTLEE

least his wife, such an attachment was deviant. Politics were best not discussed. As the Attlee children began to develop political opinions these typically reflected the conservatism of their class and time. *In this country there was the established order. A class society was accepted ... The capitalist system was as unquestioned as the solar system. It was just there!.*[2]

The Attlees were educated privately, the boys at first locally and then at boarding schools, the girls taught at home by Ellen and then abroad. Clement, perhaps because of an early illness, was taught by his mother until he was nine. Small and shy, he then followed his brother Tom to Northaw Place near Potters Bar. This prep school was obsessed with two subjects, the Bible and cricket. For Attlee the latter became a lifelong enthusiasm.

Despite his reserve he coped, and aged 13 moved to nearby Haileybury. Again he followed his brother. His record at Haileybury was unspectacular. One area where he shone was the cadet corps. The rigours of drill and discipline could compensate for his small stature. He developed a permanent and strong loyalty to the school. It was the first of several rule-governed institutions to which he would become attached. He showed some signs of academic development, reading extensively but not critically. The school was reasonably competent at preparing likely pupils for university entrance.

Attlee went up to University College Oxford in October 1901. In his time 'Univ' was a successful college, both academi-

**Haileybury** is a public school occupying imposing buildings in Hertfordshire built in 1806, with strong military traditions – Rudyard Kipling's United Services College in Westward Ho! was an offshoot from Haileybury. Its headmaster in Attlee's time was Canon Edward Lyttleton, who opposed the Boer War and whose aunt was married to the former Prime Minister W E Gladstone.

cally and in sporting achievements. It lacked the academic and worldly elitism of Balliol and the aristocratic gloss of Christ Church and Magdalen. Attlee was at ease in the company of peers from similar social backgrounds and was fortified by a paternal allowance of £200 a year. He was following a family pattern. Two brothers had already graduated from the university, and Tom was in his final year at Corpus Christi. Attlee's recollections were idyllic, an image of a town before the invasion of the motor car. Magical, almost timeless. *The Victorian age had only just ended and there was little apprehension of the troubles that lay ahead when civilisation enshrined in Oxford was to be assailed by the barbarians – Hitler and Stalin.*[3]

Attlee, at Gallipoli or on the Western Front, when faced with danger would take an imaginary stroll around Oxford streets. The idyllic image should be scrutinised, not least because of its ready endorsement by subsequent biographers. Attlee's Oxford was not timeless. Walking down the 'High' he would pass the Examination Schools. Completed in the early 1880s, it was an imposing statement of academic changes and ambitions. Many colleges extended their buildings in the late 19th century. Ironically Attlee's later socialist inspiration, William Morris, had lamented the loss of old Oxford. Change was not restricted to fabric. Attlee read Modern History. This honours school was only 30 years old. Its coverage of English History ended with the accession of Victoria. It presented, often positively, the constitutional development of Britain against a broad canvass of the rise and fall of empires. This morality tale was based on a faith in the soundness and superiority of British institutions. It provided a usable past for those who would administer an imperial state. Within this framework Attlee read widely and achieved a Second. Arthur Johnson of All Souls, a classic first-generation Modern History tutor appraised him as 'level headed, industrious ... no brilliance of style or literary gifts, but with excellent sound judgement'.[4]

Alongside his reading, Attlee became adept at billiards and prominent in a college play-reading group. But the political crises of the early 1900s left no apparent mark on him. His arrival at Oxford coincided with the last months of the Anglo-Boer war. As a schoolboy Attlee had celebrated the relief of Mafeking. Subsequent tactics against Boer guerrillas, interment camps for women and children and farm burnings, had provoked the Liberal leader Campbell-Bannerman to condemn British strategy as employing methods of barbarism. Attlee's unreflective conservatism seemed untroubled by this controversy and by subsequent arguments over tariff reform, and the employment of indentured Chinese labour in South African goldmines. *I believed in the legend of the White Man's burden and all the rest of the commonplace of imperialist idealism.*[5]

Effectively apolitical, he went down from Oxford to read for the Bar, initially at Lincoln's Inn. In the summer of 1905 he passed well in his examinations, but then spent deadening months in his father's firm. Transferring as a pupil to a commercial barrister, he was called to the Bar in March 1906. His heart was not in the law. Over the next three years he made just four court appearances. Living at home, still with his father's allowance, he sampled riding, shooting and literary discussions. But even before he was called to the Bar his life had begun to develop a new and unanticipated pattern.

One evening in October 1905, Attlee left the tedium of the Druces and Attlee office. Accompanied by his younger brother Lawrence, he took a train, not home to Putney but in the opposite direction into the East End. When they alighted a few minutes later at Stepney they had entered a world very different from the security of family, the privileges of university and the expectations of aspiring professionals. They found a working class characterised by poverty, appalling housing, casual employment and bleak expectations. The middle-class traveller had to confront, and perhaps exorcise, his prejudices and myths, and to acknowledge the limits of his own understanding. The brothers' journey ended at the Haileybury Club, founded by the public school to foster self-respect in Stepney boys, not least through military discipline. The Club was a junior section of the Territorial Army. Attlee's visits became frequent. Eighteen months later, he became manager of the Club, and left Putney to live on the premises. His commitment fitted the family tradition of public service.

His next step was at odds with this pattern, however. Confronted by the realities of working-class poverty, he rapidly rejected the conventional and consoling judgement that poverty should be attributed to individual failings and therefore necessitated individual remedies seasoned with punitive sanctions. Rather, for Attlee, individual initiatives were essential and desirable but insufficient. They required the accompaniment of political action both municipally and through the state. Political commitment was inescapable. He became a socialist.

Characteristically for Attlee, there was a fraternal influence. His brother Tom was engaged in social work in nearby Hoxton. The brothers discussed ideas and political responses. Both were attracted by 19th-century critics of industrialism, urban ugliness and competitive individualism, especially John Ruskin and William Morris. This specifically national tradition of social criticism, with the exception of Morris, was not necessarily socialist, but it shaped the outlook of many British socialists. Deeply ethical, it was far removed in style and emphasis from the Marxism available in English editions in the 1900s. The latter left no mark on Attlee's socialism. The romantic and ethical roots of his politics would endure, as would a capacity for steady and unostentatious work that was already evident at the Haileybury Club.

This specific choice was decisive. Yet for this hitherto uncritical Conservative with a Liberal father, there were other options. Sections of the Conservative Party were developing an interest in collectivism as a response to concerns about national decline. More significantly the Liberals, returned to office in the electoral landslide of 1906, were starting to develop an agenda that would be characterised by redistributive taxation, welfare reforms and a measured sensitivity towards the economic and legal demands of organised workers. The distinction between such Progressive Liberalism and ethical socialism could be unclear. Yet Attlee remained unimpressed. Immersed in the realities of working-class Stepney he saw a local council dominated by Conservatives who seemed insensitive to such experiences whilst local Liberals seemed uninfluenced by their party's new concerns. His early Conservatism perhaps immunised him against the appeal of Edwardian Liberalism. *The Liberals of the type of Asquith, Runciman and McKenna were always distasteful to me. The Liberal capitalist of the Devonport style even more so. The violent nonconforms made no appeal. The 'gentlemanly party' was to me far preferable.*[6]

Once the commitment had been made, there remained the question of its organisational expression. In 1907 the Labour Party was composed of affiliated bodies, mostly national trade unions and local trades councils, but also two significant socialist groups. The brothers sampled the Fabian Society, but were uncomfortable with the view that reforms engineered by the high-minded and the well-educated would give the working class a decent society. Clem Attlee's experiences at the Haileybury Club had persuaded him that working-class youths had the talents to make their own world in partnership with middle-class allies. For the Attlees, this judgement determined their choice – the Independent Labour Party (ILP). Early in January 1908, Clem Attlee joined the Stepney branch. This was the vital step that precipitated concern in his family. He recalled almost 30 years later: *Anyone who has been brought up in a conventional home will know the difficult adjustment necessary for the member of the family who choose another faith.*[7]

*Anyone who has been brought up in a conventional home will know the difficult adjustment necessary for the member of the family who choose another faith.*

ATTLEE

When Attlee joined the ILP, he committed himself to a party whose presence in London was meagre. From its foundation in 1893, the party's bases had been in the West Riding, Lancashire, industrial Scotland, and specific strongholds such as Leicester, Norwich and Merthyr. Its imagery and emotional discourse had affinities with religious Nonconformity. This style made slight appeal to the London working class, notable for indifference to religion and with some attachment to secularism. London socialism was expressed more often through the Social Democratic Federation (SDF), formally Marxist but often locally pragmatic. But in 1901, the SDF isolated itself from any broader alliance for Labour politics. Such inflexibility damaged the prospects for socialism in London and may help to explain Attlee's choice. Moreover his ethical route to socialism would make the ILP seem the most attractive option. As a middle-class convert, he was certainly not unique within the London ILP. Poplar and Bermondsey, Battersea and Hammersmith – all these branches included their highly-educated crusaders against poverty and injustice.

Such recruits had the resources that the party needed. The Stepney ILP was small and heavily working class. Attlee had more space in his life than most of his comrades and soon became branch secretary, as he could travel more readily to conferences. In April 1909, he was the silent Stepney delegate at the ILP's explosive Edinburgh conference, where the party's strategy was debated in vigorous and sometimes personalised exchanges. What Attlee thought about the vociferous demands for greater radicalism is unknown. His new commitment meant that his diffidence had to be conquered. The ILP was notable for its street-corner propaganda and Attlee took his share. Yet progress in Stepney remained slight. When Attlee stood for the council he polled just 69 votes.

He became visible within the wider London socialist movement. He campaigned against conditions in sweated industries, and served as an organiser for the propaganda campaign advocating the proposals of the minority report of the Royal Commission on the Poor Law. Its central theme was state responsibility for the abolition of poverty. This episode brought him into contact with the eminent Fabians, Sidney and Beatrice Webb, and with the iconic leader of East End socialism, George Lansbury. Initially the Webbs' state socialism had seemed drab at the side of William Morris' writings, but Attlee came to accept electoral politics and state action as a necessary framework for the realisation of his ideals. When Lansbury won Bow and Bromley for Labour in the December 1910 election, Attlee wrote Labour's election song and walked down the Bow Road to Mile End with a huge placard proclaiming the Labour majority. A socialist son of a London policeman recalled Attlee speaking quietly and modestly, expounding and not denouncing. Thus Herbert Morrison would remember him across decades of collaboration and rivalry.

Attlee's earned income remained sporadic although it was buttressed by £350 a year following his father's death in 1908. This bereavement allowed Attlee to abandon any pretence of a legal career. A brief and uncongenial period as secretary at the traditional university East End settlement Toynbee Hall, was followed in the hot and strikebound summer of 1911 by a stint in Somerset explaining the details of the new National Insurance Act. Eventually in 1912 he was appointed to a tutorship in Social Service at the London School of Economics. His unsuccessful rival for the post would be another long-term colleague, an extroverted product of Eton and King's, Cambridge, Hugh Dalton. Unlike Attlee he had no experience of working-class life.

Above all, Attlee established himself as a reliable worker within the ILP, both locally and more broadly within London and the South-east. His readiness to carry out unspectacular tasks was combined with mistrust of those whose socialist commitment ended with talk. His idealism was often expressed in poetry, frequently in private, but occasionally in the socialist press. Beyond his political work and continual involvement with the Haileybury Club he remained reserved, perhaps lonely. His brother Tom had married; Tom's wife Kathleen was also a socialist. The trio holidayed together in East Devon at the beginning of August 1914, where they heard the news of Britain's entry into a European war. The brothers had come to socialism together. Now temporarily they went their separate ways; Tom eventually as a conscientious objector to Wormwood Scrubs and Wandsworth Prison, Clem into the army and a record as a tough and highly competent officer.

The pre-war Stepney years were seminal to Attlee's politics. He became the man from Limehouse who had discovered the unpretentious decency and unrealised potential of the working class. Yet what were the prospects for Labour and socialism before a chauffeur drove down the wrong street in Sarajevo? Nationally the Labour Party had established a small but credible parliamentary presence in 1906 and had maintained this at both 1910 elections, but this parliamentary foothold was almost wholly dependent on Liberal willingness to allow Labour candidates free runs against Tories in a limited number of seats. Attlee might have celebrated Lansbury's December 1910 victory as a triumph for socialism, but Lansbury had not faced a Liberal opponent. Across London Labour remained weak even in working-class districts. In Stepney, despite the best efforts of Attlee and his comrades, Labour made no inroads in either borough or London County Council (LCC) elections. The possibility of running a parliamentary candidate seemed a fantasy. In part such failures highlighted the paucity of local trade unionism. Sweated trades, small workshops and casual employment, most notably on the docks, all presented obstacles to effective organisation. One institutional consequence was the absence of a local trades council. Such bodies provided a focus for Labour politics in boroughs such as Poplar, Woolwich and West Ham, allowing trade unionists and socialists to combine in successful election campaigns. In Stepney trade union weakness was in part generated by, and then left space for, ethnic rivalries between Jews, Irish Catholics and the English. Conservative and Liberal politicians played the ethnic card. In the absence of a robust labour movement, vulnerable voters could be responsive to appeals based on paternalism and prejudice.

Some auguries for London Labour seemed positive in the summer of 1914. After several false dawns a London Labour Party had been formed in May. The Social Democrats had become the dominant element in the recently-formed British Socialist Party. This organisation showed signs of shifting back towards the Labour Party. The prospect of socialist unity was complemented by rising trade union membership, a legacy of recent industrial conflicts. Yet at the parliamentary level

Labour's limited presence still depended on Liberal benevolence. A putative 1915 election might have increased pressure on this Liberal–Labour understanding but in all probability, it would have endured. When Attlee, after meeting obstacles because of his age, joined the army in September 1914, the political prospects for Labour remained obscure, but his own socialist commitment was firm.

Although he discussed his decision to join the army with his brother Tom he seems to have had no doubts. His socialism came from his East End experiences and was driven by a desire that all members of the community should have decent treatment. His earlier conservatism meant that he had never been influence by the anti-militarism and distaste for power-politics characteristic of some strands within liberalism, and which in turn had influenced the ethos of the ILP. On foreign policy Attlee was never in A J P Taylor's phrase 'a trouble maker'. Rather his community faced a challenge; he should help to find a solution. *My particular objections to doing the work cannot weigh with me if the work has to be done.*[8]

Gazetted as a lieutenant in the sixth battalion of the South Lancashires, his Territorial experience led to his command of a company. The training, predominantly of working-class Lancastrians, had affinities with his life in the East End. By June 1915, he was bound for the Turkish campaign and the tragedy of Gallipoli – heat, flies, snipers, sickness. Evacuated unconscious with dysentery this illness probably saved his life. He demanded successfully to leave the hospital ship in Malta. By his return to Gallipoli in November, heat had given way to rain, icy winds and snow. His firm and thoughtful leadership limited casualties in his Company. Just before Christmas he played a courageous part in the evacuation. Gallipoli had been Winston Churchill's strategic inspiration. Its failure damaged his career. Attlee would always believe that an imaginative strategy had been ruined by flawed execution.

The South Lancashires moved on via Alexandria to Mesopotamia. At El Hannah Attlee led his company over the top. Appropriately he carried a red flag as a warning to the supporting artillery, but he was wounded by British shrapnel as he planted his flag in an abandoned Turkish trench. Invalided to India and then to England he lobbied for a return to active service. Wounds and age counted against him, but the unremitting slaughter worked in his favour. Promoted to major, he served in France from June 1918 until wounded again in the decisive Allied push to victory. Hospitalised in Wandsworth, he was a near neighbour of his gaoled brother.

Another rule-governed institution had allowed him to develop. He built on his experiences at the Haileybury Club where he had acquired an understanding of the insecure and the bloodyminded. In the trenches efficiency, toughness and sagacity were crucial. Attlee combined empathy and discipline. He threatened to shoot a fellow officer who had lost his nerve and was refusing to go over the top, and the sight of his revolver proved persuasive. No political opponent could ever characterise him as unpatriotic; in post-war elections he stood as Major Attlee. His war experiences did not dilute his socialism. Fellow officers were left in no doubt as to his views, but his commitment to the war, his competence and the shared dangers generated tolerance. Moreover from May 1915, Labour politicians held office in successive coalition governments. State control of strategic sectors of the economy testified to the failings of unregulated capitalism in a national emergency. Attlee, like other socialists and trade unionists, hoped that methods of organisation born of war could be maintained and extended in peace.

# Chapter 2: Stepney and Parliament

Attlee returned to Stepney from the army in January 1919 to find a changed political landscape. The pre-war parliamentary franchise covering nationally about 60 per cent of adult males had gone. In its place effectively all men, and most women over 30, qualified for the vote. The change had an exceptional impact in Stepney where the previous electorate had been very small. The Labour Party had a new constitution with a socialist objective and provision for individual membership. The party reforms indicated heightened political expectations born out of the franchise expansion and dramatic growth in trade union membership. One symptom of these changes was the inaugural meeting of the Stepney Labour Party on 1 June 1918. Its secretary was a Jewish socialist; he worked closely with an Irish Catholic trade unionist. The language of economic and social interests was beginning to challenge that of ethnicity. The general election of December 1918 came too soon for these optimists. Patriotic rhetoric in the immediate aftermath of military victory, the legacy of socialist disagreements over the war and confusion about the choices on offer, all combined to defeat Labour across most of East London. But in Labour circles a belief persisted that this 'khaki' election had been a fraud perpetrated on an unprepared electorate, and retribution would follow.

In the short term, this meant organising for municipal

elections. Attlee stood for one of the two Limehouse seats on the LCC. He failed by 80 votes, but overall the party advanced within the East End. For the November 1919 borough council elections, Attlee managed Labour's campaign; he was not a candidate. The party emphasised the dire state of much East End housing and milked working-class disenchantment with the post-war record of the Lloyd George Coalition. Labour confidence was justified. November 1919 marked an electoral peak in many industrial areas. In Stepney Labour won council seats for the first time, 43 out of a possible 60. Attlee was co-opted as Mayor. His local record evoked admiration, respect and deference; his war service could reconcile those perturbed about Labour's anti-war element. Ethnic differences still threatened Labour harmony, but Attlee stood above such tensions. He recalled this first Labour municipal majority: *1/3rd Irish Catholics, 1/3rd Jews, 1/3rd English. Queer team to run.*[1]

As Mayor Attlee demonstrated strengths that would characterise his years in Downing Street. Command of procedure and effective organisation offered the essential route to reform. In council meetings he dealt sharply with the unprepared and the irrelevant. What mattered was achievement. Rate evaluations on the borough's non-residential properties were increased significantly, the proceeds funding an impressive expansion of services including maternity and child welfare, health visitors, refuse collection, libraries and public baths. Years later he would recall how the rate of infant mortality in Stepney had fallen sharply.

Attlee chaired a new association of London Labour mayors. Their term of office coincided with the ending of the post war boom. All London's mayors were invited to the Mansion

House to hear the Lord Mayor of London's modest proposals for alleviating unemployment. Attlee responded, not with customary platitudes, but with a strong appeal for more vigorous methods. More symbolically Attlee played a significant role in the deputation of London Labour mayors who met Lloyd George, again on the issue of unemployment. Battalions of the unemployed, including many ex-servicemen displaying their medals, marched to the Embankment led by their respective mayors. This demonstration by patriots whose post-war hopes had been blighted by government failure was enriched by Major Attlee with his military bearing and officer's cane leading the deputation to Downing Street. The meeting was predictably barren; the mayors emerged to battles in Whitehall between police and unemployed. Attlee intervened effectively, taking command and leading the Stepney men home.

Although Attlee opposed sterile confrontations and redundant radical rhetoric, he understood and articulated the anger of the dispossessed and the disillusioned. Once his mayoral term had ended, he was elected an Alderman. As a successful former mayor he took a radical position in the Poplar affair of 1921. This divided London Labour over fundamental issues – electoral strategy, styles of local politics and the acceptability of a calculated breach of the law in order to highlight the reality of working-class poverty. When Attlee had become first Labour mayor of Stepney, George Lansbury had become first Labour mayor of Poplar. That Labour majority similarly began to transform municipal provision, but as in Stepney rising unemployment soon became a potentially destructive challenge. Each borough was responsible for the maintenance of its own unemployed, but in impoverished Poplar, and in Stepney, Bethnal Green and Shoreditch, revenue from the rates was insufficient to fund their decent treatment. As a protest Poplar's Labour majority decided to withhold its mandatory contributions to a variety of London-wide bodies. This put them in breach of the law. The eventual imprisonment of 30 Poplar councillors in September 1921 brought publicity and an interim settlement.

Herbert Morrison, Secretary of the London Labour Party and Mayor of Hackney opposed what he, and several other Labour notables, regarded as an electorally-damaging and administratively irresponsible strategy. Morrison, supported by the major unions, won his case within the London Labour Party. But in the thoroughly working-class East End it was a different matter. Both Bethnal Green and Stepney councils backed the Poplar strategy. Attlee successfully moved that Stepney replicate the Poplar tactic unless the imprisoned councillors were released. *I have always been a constitutionalist, but the time has come when it is necessary to kick.*[2] In working-class Stepney the tactic of caution was counter-productive. *There is nothing to be gained by not adopting a bold policy. Our opponents will not be conciliated by a show of moderation.*[3]

*I have always been a constitutionalist, but the time has come when it is necessary to kick.*

ATTLEE

This opponent of the electorally judicious Morrison was also prospective parliamentary candidate for Limehouse. The constituency had been won comfortably in 1918 by Sir William Pearce, Liberal MP since 1906, a chemical manu-facturer born in Poplar. He had been amongst the minority of Liberals endorsed as Coalition candidates by Lloyd George and the Tory leader, Bonar Law. The 1918 Labour candidate had previously been the Irish Nationalist Member for Mid-Cork and was doubtless handicapped by Limehouse's ethnic divisions. In contrast Attlee's strengths were evident. He was no remote bourgeois politician who paid occasional and politically beneficial visits. He had committed himself to the East End. From early 1919 until early 1922, he lived there once again. A former member of the Haileybury Club acted as his manservant and ran his morning bath. Support of a different kind came from his agent, John Beckett, another ex-service-man who provided the panache that Attlee could not offer.

'Attlee needed careful nursing. Though he did improve, he never became an orator. His strongest cards were erudition and wit, both of which went over the heads of a Limehouse audience.'[4]

The Lloyd George Coalition collapsed in October 1922; a majority of Conservative MPs rejected the pro-Coalition sentiments of many of their own leaders. The consequent election was confused. The Tories had several prominent figures temporarily marginal-ised, while the Liberals were split into supporters of Lloyd George and Asquith. Labour therefore hoped for a signifi-cant advance. In Limehouse

**Herbert Morrison** (1888–1965) opposed British involvement in the 1914–18 war. An MP in the 1924 and 1929 parliaments, he was Minister of Transport in the second Labour government. De-feated in the 1931 election he led Labour to victory in the 1934 elections for the London County Council. He was re-elected to the Commons in 1935 but failed to defeat Attlee in an election for party leader. Prominent in the Churchill Coalition, from 1945 he was responsible for the Labour government's domestic legislation. He was less success-ful as Foreign Secretary in the government's final months.

the choice was straightforward: Attlee against Pearce. The latter stood as a Lloyd George Liberal, but like many of his colleagues had Conservative support. Attlee insisted that the real issue was Capital against Labour, a system based on exploitation or a co-operative commonwealth. His victory was clear-cut, but not as yet overwhelming.

In this November 1922 election, Labour made solid progress, 142 MPs compared with 57 in 1918. It was establishing itself in the coalfields and in working-class neighbourhoods of several major cities, not least in East London. The new Parliamentary Labour Party included leaders defeated in 1918, most notably Ramsay MacDonald and Philip Snowden, together with upper- and middle-class former Liberals who had despaired of their old party. Attlee made his own contribution to this broadening social composition. He was the first Oxford graduate to sit on the Labour benches. But a Conservative government under Bonar Law had a firm parliamentary majority. Labour might have had a credible election, but there was still a long way to go.

Labour MPs' first business after the election was to elect a chairman. The incumbent, J R Clynes, was an assiduous and cautious trade unionist. He was challenged by MacDonald who had resigned the chairmanship in August 1914, once a majority of Labour members had committed themselves to supporting the government's entry into the war. MacDonald was a leading figure in the ILP and on his day an evocative and emotional orator. He suggested a more ambitious political agenda and won the contest for the chairmanship by 61 votes to 56. Attlee voted for him. He reflected with the benefit of much hindsight, *Like others I lived to regret that vote.*[5] In November 1922 it appeared very different. MacDonald rapidly developed a status as a party leader who personified Labour aspirations. He made Attlee one of his two parliamentary secretaries.

Attlee's support for MacDonald probably reflected in part his continuing attachment to the ILP. Despite his disagreement with the party's opposition to the war, he had resumed his ILP activities in 1919. The ILP had previously been the main route for individuals like Attlee to enter the broader

Labour Party. Since the latter's new 1918 constitution permitted individual membership, the post-war ILP needed a new role. One possibility was as a socialist think-tank that would generate new ideas for the wider labour movement. Attlee became involved in this activity, engaging in discussions not least on the strengths and limitations of guild socialism. His search to give practical form to his ethical aspirations continued.

Explorations of socialist ideas were significant but were typically subordinated to the demands of parliamentary and party routines. He quickly made his maiden speech in the Commons. He spoke of East End poverty, of the waste of ability, of how the unemployed gradually became the unemployable. He stressed the lesson of wartime. In that emergency no talent had been neglected but now *you see men who were fit to be sergeant-majors in the Army – fine upstanding men – reduced to dragging along the streets with their hands out for anything they can get.*[6] Such treatment of ex-servicemen was an affront to any decent patriot. *The great mass of unemployed men are those same men who served us during the War. They are the same men who stood side by side in the trenches. They are the heroes of 1914 and 1918, though they may be pointed out as the Bolshevists of today.*[7]

*The great mass of unemployed men are those same men who served us during the War … They are the heroes of 1914 and 1918, though they may be pointed out as the Bolshevists of today.*

ATTLEE

1922 was not just the year when he entered the Commons. At the age of 39 he became a married man. For much of his life he had lived within all-male institutions – school, college, Haileybury House, the South Lancashire Regiment. In 1921 a familiar world vanished. His mother died; so did one of his sisters. The Putney house was sold; the effects were auctioned off. A longstanding support and refuge had gone.

That September Attlee holidayed in Italy with Edric Millar, a college friend of Tom Attlee and with Millar's mother and sister Violet. Violet Millar was 13 years younger than Attlee. She had been overshadowed by her academically-gifted twin sister, but her shyness melted in the company of the normally self-effacing Attlee. On their return to England he insisted that Violet, from a solidly conservative middle-class family, should hear him speaking for socialism on Hampstead Heath. Three months later in January 1922 they were married.

The result was a partnership notable for its happiness and solidarity. Vi Attlee remained the instinctively conservative woman that she had been in September 1921. Within the Labour Party affection for her was rooted not in ideological affinity but in her basic decency, especially towards children and the sick. For Attlee, his home, eventually with four children, was thoroughly separate from his political career. As with his own parents, family was sufficient. His domesticity was not invaded by political colleagues nor eroded by political anxieties. His children were educated privately; his wife had domestic help. Marriage was incompatible with living in the East End. The Attlees settled in respectable suburbia, initially in Woodford Green and from autumn 1931 in Stanmore. His wider family remained important. His brother Tom, released from gaol, settled in Cornwall and combined Christianity, bohemianism and an indifference to new technology. The brothers' lives took contrasting paths, but they remained close.

Soon after his election to the Commons Attlee ended his tutorship at the London School of Economics. He had become a full-time politician, combining Commons work, campaigning in the country and the Stepney Aldermanic bench. His Commons speeches were short on rhetoric and firm on evidence, flavoured with sharp jabs at opponents. This pattern of life seemed likely to last for a considerable time. The Conservative government did not need to call an election until 1926 or 1927. But Bonar Law resigned on health grounds in May 1923. Within six months his successor, the relatively unknown Stanley Baldwin, had called an election arguing that persistent unemployment necessitated the introduction of tariffs. This issue had divided and electorally shattered the pre-war Tories. Subsequently party leaders had prudentially avoided the issue. Baldwin's gamble demonstrated his long-standing commitment to the policy. The strategy also held out the hope of mending fences with those senior Conservatives who had been rebuffed over the fall of the Coalition.

In the short term the gamble failed. The Conservatives lost some urban seats, mostly to Labour. In suburban and rural areas where Labour was weak, the uneasily reunited Liberals made impressive and sometimes improbable gains. The outcome was a hung parliament. The Conservatives remained the largest party, while Labour improved their position by 49 seats and remained ahead of the Liberals by a margin of 33. When the Commons met in January 1924 Labour combined with almost all Liberal MPs to defeat the Conservatives. The result was the first Labour government under MacDonald. Major Attlee, who had strengthened his electoral position in Limehouse, became Under-Secretary at the War Office.

His immediate colleagues were both miners' members. Stephen Walsh from Lancashire, first elected in 1906, was senior minister and did not query the views of his military advisors. The Financial Secretary, Jack Lawson, was a Durham man who had served in the army. He was regarded as the archetypal moderate north-eastern miners' representative. Especially in the circumstances of a minority government, this triumvirate was unlikely to take radical initiatives. Attlee acquired his first awareness of the workings of a government department; in the Commons he presented departmental briefs with predictable efficiency.

His ministerial performance was characteristic of much of the government's work. Parliamentary arithmetic seemed an insuperable obstacle to controversial measures and inhibited much discussion of whether ministers had the inclination or understanding to act radically anyway. The best that could be hoped for was competence, a demonstration of Labour's ability to govern, tempered with the realistic expectation that the government's life would be short. Defeat in Parliament came early in October 1924, precipitating the third general election in less than two years.

The government fell on the issue of Campbell case. Both Conservatives and Liberals claimed that ministers had interfered improperly in the planned prosecution of a Communist journalist J R Campbell for sedition. The wider backdrop was the prospect of an Anglo-Soviet Treaty. The election was notable for Conservative and some Liberal hysteria over Labour's alleged tenderness towards Bolshevism. The finale was the publication in the *Daily Mail*, a few days before polling, of the so-called Zinoviev Letter. Now dismissed as a forgery, this document outlined the Communist International's revolutionary agenda for Britain. The scurrility of the campaign had minimal impact in Limehouse. Attlee's vote increased slightly; his majority fell by even less. Nationally the Conservative majority was massive, largely at the expense of the Liberals. Labour lost 40 seats, but ran more candidates and increased their vote by over a million.

Back in opposition Attlee became an even more assiduous Commons speaker. He made 48 contributions in 1924–5 and 40 in 1925–6. Although his range of topics was extensive; his most substantial speeches came on rating and electricity supply where his Stepney experiences gave him expertise.

He was not in the front rank of Labour parliamentarians but he was regarded as an unspectacularly valuable and well-informed member of Labour's second generation. After 1924, his involvement in the Independent Labour Party declined. Increasingly the ILP became dominated by critics of MacDonald and of what they dismissed as Labour caution. For Attlee, as for many others, this change was unacceptable. He gradually loosened his ties with the organisation through which he had entered politics.

A more immediate demand for solidarity faced Attlee in the spring of 1926. Miners in several coalfields faced draconian wage cuts, and the Trades Union Congress (TUC) called out members of several unions in support of the Miners' Federation. Attlee was more involved in the consequential nine-day General Strike than many Labour parliamentarians. As chairmen of Stepney Borough Electricity Committee he led negotiations with the Electrical Trades Union. The unions agreed that light should be supplied to the borough, but power should be available only to hospitals. Since the lighting supply could often be used for power, Attlee agreed that power workers could end all supplies to any transgressor. One firm suffered this penalty and subsequently took out a civil action for conspiracy against Attlee and other Labour members of the committee. The defendants lost and damages of £300 were found against Attlee, but eventually the judgement was revoked on appeal. The episode demonstrated Attlee's pragmatism as a negotiator – Stepney Conservatives had supported the arrangement – but he did not flinch from the more radical implications.

On the broader issue of the General Strike Attlee was sceptical. He saw the TUC policy as muddled but admired the fortitude of the miners as they battled in isolation only to experience crushing defeat after seven months. He welcomed the discrediting of the belief that industrial struggle might offer a shortcut to radical changes. Rather, the parliamentary road was unavoidable, whatever the frustrations. His assessment was typical of most Labour politicians in the 1920s. Whatever doubts there had been about MacDonald's leadership after the 1924 defeat were suppressed in pursuit of electoral success. There is no reason to believe that Attlee dissented from this consensus. Then late in 1927, his career took an unexpected turn.

The Government of India Act had been passed by the Lloyd George Coalition in 1919. At provincial level elected legislative councils would have some powers, but governors would retain control of justice, police and finance. India as a whole would have a largely elected bicameral legislature with limited powers. Much power would be retained by the Viceroy and by his executive council where Indians were in a minority. The British had presented the package as a significant reform. Indian politicians had rejected it as trivial. The Act had provided that a commission be set up to assess the efficacy of the reforms. In November 1927 the Conservative Secretary of State for India, Lord Birkenhead, announced the Commission's early advent. The Chairman would be the Liberal politician, Sir John Simon. He had become a target for Labour hostility because of his denunciation of the General Strike as illegal. Four of the Commission's members would be Conservative; two would be Labour. Some Labour possibilities proved unavailable, so eventually the places were taken by the South Wales miners' member Vernon Hartshorn and Clement Attlee. Any involvement by Labour politicians was viewed sceptically within some sections of the party. There was suspicion that the Baldwin government desired a cautious report that would stifle pressure for Dominion status. Attlee was not an obvious choice. He had briefly been a patient in a Bombay hospital in 1916, and his glimpses of India had been limited to the more Europeanised sections of the city: in hospital he had passed the time by reading an Arnold Bennett novel. Perhaps Attlee's distaste for radical rhetoric was seen as advantageous. He might find a sober report appropriate. He had paid little attention to Indian issues and had no preconceptions beyond an endorsement of his party's support for eventual self-government.

The Commission visited India twice – a preliminary visit from January to April 1928, and a second one to take evidence beginning in October 1928 and returning the following April. Its exclusively British membership produced a boycott by many politically active Indians. *We saw the worst side of the Congress Party. We probably underestimated the extent of political intelligence and vigour.*[8] Simon stuck to his task. This consummate lawyer noted with approval Attlee's intellectual quality and efficiency. Attlee was the more active of the Labour members. He recalled Hartshorn as delightful and humorous, but not over-addicted to work.[9] Attlee was impressed by the complexity of the issues. He felt that the Commission's restrictive focus on political change was a severe limitation, since economic and social inequalities were crippling. Above all there was Attlee the pragmatist. *India was not a tabula rasa but a paper that has been much scribbled over.*[10] Amidst the novel complexities was the reassuringly familiar: Attlee attended an Old Haileyburian dinner at Rawalpindi.

He returned from the Commission's second spell in India to the May 1929 election. The result was his best performance yet in Limehouse. For the first time Labour became the largest party in the House of Commons and formed another minority government. Neither Attlee nor Hartshorn joined the new administration. The Simon Report had yet to be written. Nevertheless Attlee's omission seems to have irritated him.

The commissioners soon found the purpose of their work undermined. Faced with rising Indian discontent, in October 1929 the Viceroy Lord Irwin announced the calling of a round-table conference of Indians and Britons. He proposed that the MacDonald government publicly commit itself to Dominion status. The government rapidly did so. The response of the Indian National Congress was to demand complete independence. The Simon Commission's labours had been marginalised.

Attlee was annoyed. His involvement in the Commission had attracted some Labour criticism and had disrupted his family life. Characteristically he persevered with the report. This was published without any note of dissent in June 1930. The first instalment, largely the work of Simon, was an analytical survey. The second contained the recommendations. A new constitution should give more powers to Indian provincial government but governors and the Viceroy should retain vetoes. Attlee's support for the findings and his significant part in their production distanced him from many on the left. The socialist intellectual, Harold Laski, overtly attacking Simon also might have been targeting a second contributor to the report. 'You cannot deal with the hopes of a people as though they were studies in logic.'[11]

With the completion of the Simon Report Attlee entered the government in May 1930. Labour members' early optimism had withered in the face of rapidly rising unemployment. Trade unions and backbenchers demanded an effective response, preferably a reduction in the level of unemployment. If this was not possible, then at least the unemployed should be treated decently. Yet most ministers, especially the Chancellor of the Exchequer Philip Snowden, remained confined within the rigours of Treasury opinion. In May 1930 the evident failure of Jimmy Thomas, the minister responsible for employment policy, precipitated a political crisis. One of MacDonald's junior ministers, Sir Oswald Mosley, resigned from the government after the rejection of his own proposals for reducing unemployment. Party managers placated worried backbenchers. MacDonald moved Thomas to the Dominions Office replacing him with Hartshorn. Attlee took Mosley's post as Chancellor of the Duchy of Lancaster.

His remit was to advise the government on a variety of issues. He worked harmoniously with the newly-appointed Agricultural Minister, Christopher Addison. Attlee's praise indicated his own criteria for effectiveness in office. *Addison has turned out to be about the best and most rigorous minister we've got. He knows to make his department work and can work with others, being always ready to take suggestions and set aside preconceived ideas in favour of others.*[12]

Attlee was less enamoured of his membership of the recently-created Economic Advisory Council. Here, ministers, economists, trade unionists and businessmen discussed the diagnosis of and prescriptions for the economic crisis. One consequence of its often-inconclusive discussions was Attlee's preparation of a paper on the Problems of British Industry. He was advised by the economist, Colin Clark. The paper emphasised rationalisation, in other words the concentration of production in more efficient units. The policy should be pursued more vigorously thorough a new Ministry of Industry.

Characteristically for this government none of this became effective policy. Unemployment rose further in the winter of 1930–1. Sir Charles Trevelyan resigned as President of the Board of Education, frustrated both by denominational squabbles over educational reform and the general passivity of the government. In the resulting reshuffle, Attlee was given his own department, the Post Office. He enjoyed running a department and began to investigate ways of reducing centralisation.

On the broader political stage these months in the spring and summer of 1931 brought mixed signals. Despite economic depression and parliamentary vulnerability the government had survived. However, poor by-election results suggested that its longer-term prospects were bleak. Liberals also feared an early election and ministers hoped that enough Liberals would support the government on a regular basis. As yet the attempt to balance between the priorities of the labour movement and the strictures of the economically orthodox had been reasonably successful. In March 1931 the government had bought time in the Commons by agreeing to a committee under Sir George May to review public expenditure. Through all these uncertainties and with a seemingly intractable unemployment problem, Attlee, like other ministers, suppressed his doubts. In part this was a simple issue of loyalty to a beleaguered government. Moreover, alternatives seemed unattractive. Trevelyan's resignation had provoked backbench hostility. ILP critics of the government were few in number, increasingly isolated and ineffective. Mosley and a very few supporters had quit Labour to form a New Party of ambiguous identity. Endurance seemed a credible response. Small reforms might be secured.

The May Report was published at the end of July 1931. Senior ministers hoped to use the summer recess to digest its recommendations, and then to construct a response to lay before Parliament in the autumn. The Report, having painted a gruesome portrait of the financial situation, proposed swingeing cuts in public expenditure. This agenda in itself posed a serious challenge to ministerial ingenuity, but the challenge rapidly became a deep and immediate crisis.

Serious difficulties within the Austrian and German banking systems led to a run on sterling. Britain had returned to the Gold Standard in 1925; gold began to haemorrhage out of the City of London. Senior ministers faced demands for rapid and thorough implementation of the May Report, in order to restore confidence and to maintain the parity of the pound. Discussions in Cabinet were complex, ambiguous and fraught. On 20 August MacDonald and Snowden faced the hostility of the TUC General Council, most notably the TUC's General Secretary Walter Citrine and the Transport Workers' leader Ernest Bevin. This experience of trade union dissent greatly influenced Arthur Henderson, not just the Foreign Secretary, but also Party Secretary. He had a strong sense of the necessity for a harmonious party–union relationship and subsequently served as the focus for those Cabinet members opposed to the political consequences of retrenchment. Three days later the government disintegrated. Its final symbolic act came when the Cabinet divided eleven to nine in favour of a 10 per cent cut in unemployment benefit.

**Ramsay MacDonald** (1866–1937) was born in Lossiemouth, Morayshire. Initially a Liberal, he joined the ILP in 1894 and in 1900 became Secretary of the Labour Representation Committee. Principal architect of the new party, he was elected to the Commons in 1906. He opposed British entry into the war in 1914 and lost his seat in 1918. An MP again from 1922 he was Labour Prime Minister in 1924 and from 1929–31. On the first occasion he was also Foreign Secretary. In August 1931, faced with financial crisis, he formed a National Government overwhelmingly defeated his old party in an election and remained as Prime Minister until 1935. (See *MacDonald* by Kevin Morgan, in this series.)

This drama was played out within a small group. Most

Labour politicians were on holiday and were poorly informed. Attlee and his family were enjoying the English seaside at ultra-respectable Frinton. When he relieved a message asking him to meet MacDonald on 24 August, he was unsure of its significance. *The political scene is full of alarms and excursions, and what will be the upshot God knows. I have been summoned to see the PM tomorrow, but whether on certain GPO matters or on the general situation I know not.*[13]

Arriving in London, he met Hugh Dalton, a junior Foreign Office minister. They discussed the crisis over lunch. Dalton recorded how Attlee criticised MacDonald for indecision and an inferiority complex, and Snowden as a block on progress. The junior ministers' meeting had been called to inform them about the crisis, and perhaps to tell them of a salary cut. By the morning of the 24th it was known that the Labour government would resign, but at the meeting MacDonald told the ministers that he had agreed to head a cross-party National Government. Only two of his audience questioned him, Dalton and Attlee. The latter's query was characteristically brief. *What about the rentiers?*[14] If the crisis necessitated equality of sacrifice how would this affect those who lived off unearned income?

MacDonald had the support of only a dozen Labour backbenchers. These were typically middle class, university educated and recent entrants to the Commons. In contrast Attlee's roots went deep within the party. Loyalty was fundamental, just like Gallipoli. Attlee subsequently justified his decision with a military comparison. *Some of you have been soldiers no doubt. You will know then that there is only one occasion when a soldier is justified in disobeying orders. That is when his senior officer goes over to the enemy.*[15]

Yet MacDonald's dominance over the party had endured until this final crisis. Many Labour MPs broke with him only with regret and pain. Their letters to him expressed respect and sometimes affection. In contrast Attlee's valediction was characteristically correct. *While I have no doubt that the action that you have taken has been dictated solely in the endeavour to serve the country, I personally must take my stand with those members of the Cabinet who disagree with the course adopted.*[16]

To his brother Tom he articulated both anger and realism. *Things are pretty damnable. I fear we are in for a regime of false economy and a general attack on the workers' standard of life ... The real trouble to my mind has been the failure of Snowden all through to face the financial situation. He has always rather slavishly followed City opinion, while JRM has been far too prone to take his views from bankers and big business.*[17]

Labour moved to the left, seeking to combine socialist rhetoric with a credible programme. Early in September Attlee joined several leading members of the parliamentary party on a Finance and Trade Committee. The recent Labour Cabinet had accepted much economic orthodoxy, but had revolted against the political costs. Now this group sharpened differences with the new National Government. Their hostility to the new administration's programme of economies emphasised the principle of ability to pay. But the committee still stressed a commitment to sound finance. Recent traumas compelled however the recognition that a socialist government in a capitalist system inevitably faced thorough opposition from the old order. One response was an increased emphasis on the extensive state control of finance and industry.

Acerbic and sometimes vitriolic exchanges in the Commons deepened the gulf between Labour loyalists and those who had joined the National Government. This process of polarisation discomforted Labour's new leader Arthur Henderson. A crisis administration, formed to protect the Gold Standard, found itself forced off gold without the predicted apocalypse. Labour MPs were divided over the extent to which this government action should be criticised. Attlee voted with the more radical element. Pressure grew within the National Government for a quick election. Conservative supporters might differ from Liberal allies and the few Labour renegades on policy, but all could unite to denounce Labour as incompetent and unpatriotic, and the trade unions as would-be dictators. Despite the efforts of some historians at rehabilitation, the October 1931 election was a moment when calumny and self-righteousness embraced. For the first time Labour faced a united opposition. In the 1920s the electoral system, allied to the complexities of three-party politics, had given Labour an exaggerated parliamentary strength in comparison with its popular support. In 1931 the reverse happened. The 287 seats won in 1929 plummeted to just 46 plus five ILP rebels and one Labour independent. Most of the 46 victors were returned in the coalfields. Eight came from London; these included Attlee who was successful in Limehouse by 551 votes.

Labour's first generation of leaders had virtually vanished. MacDonald, Snowden and Thomas had shared in the National triumph that had massacred their former party. Henderson had been defeated. From the Labour Cabinet that had fragmented two months earlier only Attlee's old East End comrade George Lansbury survived. Five defeated members of that Cabinet had been born in the 1880s, Attlee's decade. They had been viewed as the party's rising stars. Amongst the junior ministers, the transparently ambitious Hugh Dalton had been defeated by a margin little greater than that of Attlee's victory. Most of the other survivors were trade unionists, almost all solid loyalists who had rarely spoken in the Commons. Much more distinctive was Sir Stafford Cripps, the former Solicitor General. This talented and rich lawyer had only brief experience of parliamentary and broader Labour politics. Amidst this electoral devastation the septuagenarian Lansbury became leader and Attlee his deputy. Cripps intellectually resourceful and thoroughly committed came in to form a triumvirate. The significance of these weeks for Attlee can hardly be overestimated. Faced with the consequences of a political crisis in which he had not participated, he instinctively and unambiguously sided with the bulk of the parliamentary party and the trade unions. He was involved in discussions that began to transform Labour's programme. His survival of the electoral cull suddenly made him a senior figure in a small parliamentary party.

This eminence might be temporary, but it should be placed in the context of a significant shift in party opinion. That MacDonald had ever led a National Government was bad enough; that he had played a leading role in the electoral near-obliteration of the party he had done so much to build guaranteed selective Labour amnesia about the party's own past. For many such forgetting was a denial of their earlier admiration. MacDonald's style had personified Labour's advance in the 1920s. Now it was dismissed as flamboyant and dishonest. Such leaders could not be trusted.

Trade union experience of the 1929 government had been one of disillusion by instalment. The government's disintegration had happened when dominant TUC figures, especially Ernest Bevin, had decided that the strategy of defending the mediocre to prevent the worst had failed. The result was not a trade union determination to control Labour politicians, but rather a concern to establish a relationship in which politicians would respond to trade union priorities with understanding and sensitivity. A prevalent trade union diagnosis of the disaster was that responsibility lay with the 'intellectuals' – an anathema applicable to MacDonald and Snowden but equally to Mosley and to the irreconcilables of the ILP. This indictment could extend to those who had stayed with Labour but whose penchant for political manoeuvres and posturing could be interpreted as evidence of unreliability.

After 1931, the political balance within the Labour party was exceptional. Under MacDonald the parliamentarians had dominated. Key extra-parliamentary institutions, the National Executive Committee and the Party Conference, had been subordinate. Now the parliamentary party was small and composed largely of unknowns. Ambitious politicians of Labour's second generation, especially Dalton and Herbert Morrison, attempted to maintain their influence through their seats on the National Executive. This membership and their talent and industry gave them leading roles in the development of a party programme. Attlee played little part in this exercise. He did not sit on the National Executive until 1934. Understandably Morrison and Dalton viewed their work as vital for the party's future. Confident of personal success at the next election they belittled the style and achievements of the parliamentary leadership.

Yet the four years following the 1931 election were crucial in the strengthening of Attlee's reputation, especially amongst the small group of Labour MPs. He spoke very frequently in debates and spent long hours in the chamber supporting colleagues who had to tackle unfamiliar subjects and who often lacked confidence. Here was another example of the unglamorous supportive work evident at Haileybury House and in the trenches. As a campaigning speaker he was no star turn, especially in contrast with the iconic Lansbury, but his ethical socialism flavoured his pragmatism. The shell-shocked party needed optimism. The triumvirate in their contrasting styles could provide this. *George, Stafford and I endeavour to give them the pure milk of the word, and no blooming gradualism and palliatives.*[18]

Above all Attlee epitomised the post-1931 ethos. His low-key style contrasted with the official memory of MacDonald. He obviously lacked the self-seeking ambition and vanity that could arouse trade union suspicions.

*George, Stafford and I endeavour to give them the pure milk of the word, and no blooming gradualism and palliatives.*

ATTLEE

Attlee's early response to the disaster suggested a personal shift to the left. Even before the collapse of the Labour government he had become involved in a new group founded by the Oxford academic G D H Cole, the Society for Socialist Inquiry and Propaganda (SSIP). This was envisaged as a forum that might develop credible socialist policies. Its fate was determined by the consequences of the ILP's final break with the Labour Party in July 1932. Many within the ILP baulked at this isolation and sought a new organisational home within the Labour Party. The outcome in the autumn of 1932 was the coming together of this element with the SSIP to form the Socialist League. The League became strongly identified with Cripps who was shifting strongly to the left. It developed a Marxist discourse and eventually became established as a critical left minority within the party. For a short period Attlee was involved. His outlook was evident at the party's 1932 Leicester conference, the peak of radical reaction to the previous year's disaster. Attlee strongly supported a resolution that the next Labour government, majority or minority, should implement a socialist programme. *I think the events of last year have shown that no further progress can be made in seeking to get crumbs from the rich man's table.*[19]

Attlee and Cripps were close colleagues. When Lansbury

became seriously ill at the end of 1933, Attlee felt that Cripps was Lansbury's natural successor, and should become acting leader. Cripps discreetly paid £500 into party funds allowing Attlee to take on the task. But Cripps became more committed to his personal variant on the Socialist League outlook, and was viewed by some within the party as an electoral liability. Attlee typically remained close to the party's centre of gravity. At Labour's 1934 Southport conference, the Socialist League's attempts to radicalise the party programme – *For Socialism and Peace* – met with thorough rejection. Attlee was dismissive. *I wish people would not always want to be strafing their friends instead of their enemies.*[20] Even so the programme was the most radical Labour had yet produced.

The rhetorical revivalism of the platform testified to Attlee's socialist commitment, but international developments and expectations promoted pessimistic assessments of what was feasible. In April 1933, with Hitler strengthening his regime and the Austrian Left under a threat that would soon be tragically realised, he saw little basis for optimism in Europe. *I fear Social democracy in Germany is down and out for a generation and Austria is likely to be crushed. Thus all Europe with the possible exception of Czechoslovakia that lies East of the Rhineland and south of the Baltic is lost to democracy. It raises most difficult problems for our movement.* He rejected one frequent source of encouragement for the 1930s Left. *I think that Russia is in a bad way economically and that the policy of world revolution based on Russian support has really failed and that the communist movement cannot save, but can only injure the cause.* As yet he was uncertain about the impact of the recently-installed Roosevelt administration in Washington, but wondered if the best way forward was a movement working on lines of western democracy in the British Empire and the USA. Although *capitalism ... may come down with a crash, international socialism was in no state to take its place. More likely capitalism will pull itself round transforming itself considerably in the process.*[21] Attlee's pragmatism was once again publicly evident on Indian affairs. With Conservatives arguing bitterly about Indian reform, for 18 months from the spring of 1933 he sat on a time-consuming parliamentary committee. Its recommendations became a basis for the 1935 Government of India Act. Attlee suppressed any points of difference. On this imperial issue he strove for consensus.

Despite the industry of Attlee and his colleagues, Labour's recovery from the trough of 1931 was limited and uneven. Financial difficulties were only partially addressed through economies and drives for new members. Organisational weakness was evident in some by-election campaigns. The party regained several seats lost in 1931; its support peaked late in 1933. Although confidence revived early in 1935, MacDonald's belated replacement as Prime Minister by Baldwin, and the patriotic emotion engendered by the Silver Jubilee, suggested a government recovery. The extent of government support depended very much on the retention of the large number of Liberal voters who had gone National, not Labour in 1931. The Labour Party faced a stiff electoral challenge. In autumn 1935 it suddenly faced a leadership crisis.

Lansbury's leadership was destroyed publicly and brutally by Ernest Bevin at the party conference in October 1935. The occasion was a debate on international affairs in the context of Mussolini's imminent invasion of Abyssinia. The crisis required the Labour Party to take a clear position on the imposition of sanctions against Italy by the League of Nations. Ultimately this could mean the use of military force. The policy was backed by both the party and the TUC. In contrast Lansbury maintained his long-standing pacifism. Attlee's contribution to the debate emphasised that joining the League of Nations carried a commitment to support sanctions, just as becoming a member of a trade union meant an obligation to strike in certain circumstances. While Lansbury stressed the right of individual conscience Attlee accepted the logic of a commitment to collective action. In the debris left by the debate Labour MPs reluctantly accepted Lansbury's resignation. Attlee once again became caretaker leader.

# Chapter 3: Party Leader and the War Cabinet

The general election was held on 14 November 1935. Victory for the National Government was anticipated although its extent was a surprise. The government made much of its verbal backing for League of Nations' policy on Abyssinia. Ministers could point to an economic recovery, albeit limited and occupationally and geographically uneven. Labour secured 154 seats, similar to its standing in 1922 and 1924, but with a higher share of the vote. It strengthened its dominance in the coalfields and showed some recovery in cities in Scotland and the north of England, and in working-class London. Elsewhere in the south the party failed badly. The formerly Liberal vote stayed strongly with the government. Labour's base was heavily working class, but only within sections of the working class. The electoral challenge for a new leader was forbidding.

Such a defeat would have meant Lansbury's resignation anyway. The limited electoral advance brought back many of Labour's senior figures. Arthur Greenwood, Minister of Health in the 1929 government, had been returned at a by-election in 1932. Three more of the younger ex-Cabinet ministers returned in 1935, Morrison, A V Alexander and Tom Johnston. There was one tragic absence: Willie Graham, industrious and honest, perhaps a Scottish Attlee, had died aged 45 in 1932. But Hugh Dalton, a conspiratorial extrovert, was also back.

From an older generation Clynes, who had briefly been MacDonald's predecessor, ruled himself out on grounds of age. Cripps had become unacceptable to the electorally nervous and to trade unionists suspicious of intellectuals' irresponsibility. Alexander and Johnston showed no interest and probably had an accurately pessimistic view of their prospects. Dalton certainly had ambitions, but for the moment, volunteered his services as Morrison's indiscreet campaign manager.

Herbert Morrison was widely regarded as the favourite. A thorough politician of working-class origins, an effective organiser who was interested in ideas, he could point to two major achievements. He had been a successful Minister of Transport in the 1929 government, and as a late entrant to the Cabinet he represented achievement in a frequently disappointing government. In 1934, he had led Labour to its first ever victory in elections to the London County Council. The success was a triumph for Morrison's strategy of a broad and practical cross-class appeal and rested on the organisational capacity of the London Labour Party. The subsequent administration of London provided a fine example of municipal Labour in action. But there were weaknesses. He had long been an organisational hammer of the left. There were scores to be settled. In the 1931 crisis he had voted in favour of cutting unemployment benefit. Rumours that he had been tempted to join the National Government were probably well founded. His London achievements and preoccupations allowed detractors to paint him unfairly as parochial. His time in the Commons had been brief, barely three years, and the leader was elected by MPs. Above all, perhaps, he had attracted the antipathy of Ernest Bevin, possibly because of a perceived personal slight. There had been policy clashes.

Morrison had opposed legislation on London transport backed by Bevin's union in 1924. More recently there had been a complex quarrel over the status of trade unionists on the boards of public corporations. Whatever the cause, Bevin's enmity was all too apparent. Morrison could be stigmatised as insensitive to trade union interests.

This charge could not be made against Arthur Greenwood. He too had been a ministerial success in 1929–31. Unlike Morrison he had stood resolutely on what became the side of the angels. He had opposed cuts in unemployment benefits long before the publication of the May Report, and in the tortuous Cabinet discussions of August 1931, he had been one of the first and strongest critics of substantial expenditure cuts. Born into the working class but socially mobile through education, he headed the party's Research Department. Where Morrison aroused controversy and strong feelings Greenwood conciliated not least with the unions. Like Attlee his Commons career had begun in 1922; it had been interrupted only briefly in 1931. He had one serious drawback, however: by the mid-1930s he had become an alcoholic.

At first sight Attlee could appear the least qualified. He had never sat in Cabinet, although given the record of 1929–31 this need not be disadvantageous. His terseness could seem a virtue in the reaction against MacDonald. Unlike Greenwood he was no habitué of the Commons bars. His independence of cliques, social and political, could facilitate party cohesion. Above all, those who had served in the 1931 Parliament knew his virtues – the long hours on the Opposition front bench, the coaching of sometimes reluctant, often unsure back-benchers, his mugging-up of unfamiliar subjects so that the party could mount some sort of show against the entrenched National Government. Major Attlee had once more done his duty. As stand-in leader for the election he had done nothing wrong. He could benefit from Labour's ethic of not doing an incumbent out of a job.

Dalton characteristically and doubtless vociferously proclaimed that the choice was between a non-entity, a drunkard and Herbert. The choice was made by Labour MPs on 26 November 1935. On the first ballot Attlee, nominated by two miners' members, received 58 votes, Morrison 44 and Greenwood 33. In the second ballot, with Greenwood's votes available, Attlee's vote rose by 30 and Morrison's by only four. The impressive discipline of the Greenwood contingent led to Morrison and Dalton claiming in their memoirs that at least some of the disposition of Greenwood's vote was decided at a Freemasons' meeting. A leading figure in the lodge was the parliamentary party's salaried secretary Scott Lindsay, one of Greenwood's drinking cronies. This was at most a peripheral factor. Relatively few MPs attended the allegedly crucial Lodge meeting. More significantly the initial supporters of Attlee who probably included most of the Miners' Group, preferred Attlee's unostentatious fidelity to the party and his respect for the conventions of the wider labour movement.

Dalton dismissed the result as wretched and disheartening: 'a little mouse shall lead them.' Beatrice Webb labelled Attlee 'irreproachable but colourless', but she also acknowledged that 'Attlee, the neutral and least disliked member of the Front Bench, may be better than Morrison the dictator of policy'.[1] Attlee acknowledged that his initial election was for one session only. Until the outbreak of war his tenure had a provisional character. However, Morrison, with a remarkable flair for scoring own goals in his pursuit of the leadership, immediately strengthened Attlee's position. He refused nomination for the Deputy Leader's post and devoted his time to the LCC. Instead Greenwood, acceptable but often incapable, took the job, thereby lessening the pressure on Attlee.

Despite the decisive election defeat the party largely stuck by the programme of economic planning, public ownership and welfare that had been drawn up in the early 1930s. Under Attlee's leadership there was no anxious revisiting of proposals to assess what revisions might strengthen Labour's electoral appeal. *Labour's Immediate Programme*, published in March 1937, clarified what a Labour government would do. The list of industries to be nationalised was limited to coal, power, transport and armaments. This clarification was complemented by Attlee's book, *The Labour Party in Perspective*. This emphasised both party's and author's commitment to a socialist commonwealth. For Attlee clear exposition and commitment to principle were essential.

Attlee's faith in the electoral viability of such an appeal would be tested at an election in 1939 or 1940. However the deteriorating situation in Europe soon came to dominate Labour Party discussions. The Spanish Civil War became emblematic for the European left. When Spanish generals led a revolt of conservative Spain against the elected Republican government in July 1936, the first response of both the TUC and the Labour Party was non-intervention. This policy shadowed the position of the recently-elected Popular Front government in France. It also indicated the assessment of some senior figures, notably Ernest Bevin and Hugh Dalton, that Spain was a peripheral issue. Early and overwhelming evidence that Germany and Italy were supplying the rebels with arms and combatants produced a speedy reversal of Labour policy. In December 1937 Attlee and some colleagues visited the Republican forces outside Madrid. He admired the cool courage of the Spaniards. He visited the International Brigade *in a bitter cold wind … the men drawn up in the square of a village with torches held all round*. One company became the Major Attlee Company. On his return he denied that the conflict was between fascism and communism. *The real contest in Spain is between liberty and tyranny ... Continued acquiescence in a one-sided non-intervention has made the British Government an accessory to the attempt to murder democracy in Spain.*[2]

*Continued acquiescence in a one-sided non-intervention has made the British Government an accessory to the attempt to murder democracy in Spain.*

ATTLEE

The growing threat from Nazi Germany posed a formidable challenge for the Labour Party with its strong traditions of anti-militarism and distaste for power-politics. Attlee had never been affected by the pacifistic traditions of radical liberalism, but he supported the established policy of pursuing collective security through the League of Nations whilst reducing national armaments. However by 1936, following the Abyssinian debacle, reliance on the power of the League lacked credibility. The issue of a specifically British response to German demands had become inescapable, and this inevitably raised the question of support for any rearmament initiated by the National Government.

One symbolic issue concerned the annual votes by Labour MPs against the Service Estimates. Dalton, an advocate of a more robust attitude to defence, failed to end this practice in July 1936. At that autumn's party conference, divisions and animosities amongst Labour leaders became apparent in a foreign affairs debate. Attlee's private verdict suggested that as yet, he maintained the official party position.

*There is a good deal of sore feeling over Hitler which is not without justification, but makes some people want to support Government policy on armaments which is stupid. The Government have no clear foreign policy and their armaments policy is futile and wasteful.*[3]

In July 1937 the executive of the parliamentary party once again endorsed the traditional policy on the Estimates. Attlee presented this to a meeting of Labour MPs. However, they rejected such opposition by 45 votes to 39. International developments and lobbying had made an impact. Attlee was not embarrassed. He defined his leadership role as reflecting party opinion. *Unless acquiescence in the views of the majority conflicts with my conscience I shall fall into line.*[4]

Thereafter as the *Anschluss* with Austria was succeeded by the dismemberment of Czechoslovakia, a British guarantee to Poland and abortive negotiations with the Soviet Union, Attlee and his party could claim retrospectively to be amongst those who had seen through the naivety of appeasement. For Attlee disagreements became sharper once Baldwin, whom he respected, had been succeeded by Neville Chamberlain in May 1937. Dislike was mutual. Attlee felt that Chamberlain's personalised foreign policy combined anachronistic attitudes and incompetence – *just an imperialist of the old school, but without much knowledge of foreign affairs or appreciation of the forces at work.*[5] Nevertheless Labour sentiments still needed judicious management. Late in April 1939 the government introduced a bill for military conscription. The unions feared its extension to industry and Attlee opposed the measure as divisive.

Despite the failure of the government's policy on European security, evident in the final destruction of Czechoslovakia in March 1939, Labour had little reason for electoral optimism. By-elections did not indicate any hope of a Labour majority at the next general election. Pessimism about Labour's chances, alarm about the international situation, a desire to attract Liberal voters and the Communist strategy of a Popular Front produced a variety of proposals for a broader electoral alliance culminating in a final initiative by Cripps early in 1939. Such attempts reawakened familiar spectres – fear of entanglements with other political groups, suspicion of Communist motives and criticism of Cripps as a rich intellectual who could not be trusted. The electoral benefit of such a strategy was not obvious.

Attlee had become highly critical of Cripps. *He is so absolutely convinced that the policy that he puts forward for the time being is absolutely right and will listen to no arguments.*[6] The rejection of Cripps' agenda and his subsequent expulsion from the party terminated the debate but offered no solution to the electoral problem. Attlee articulated a straightforward faith that a clear-cut socialist appeal would be more attractive than any scheme of electoral co-operation. The truth was that in the summer of 1939 neither option offered much hope of early success.

During several months of that critical year Attlee was ill with a prostate problem. He barely featured at the party conference at the end of May. When Hitler's troops invaded Poland at the beginning of September he was convalescing by the sea in North Wales. When Labour MPs combined with Conservative critics to harry Chamberlain over the government's hesitant response to German aggression, it was Arthur Greenwood, not Attlee, who responded forcefully to the Tory Imperialist Leo Amery's challenge to 'Speak for England'.

**Sir (Richard) Stafford Cripps (1889–1952)** was the nephew of Beatrice Webb and son of a Conservative MP who later sat in the first two Labour Cabinets. Educated at Winchester and University College London he became a very successful lawyer. Recruited as Labour's Solicitor-General in 1930 he survived the 1931 disaster and moved sharply to the left .This shift culminated in his expulsion from the party in 1939. A successful wartime minister, he re-joined the party and served in the Attlee government at the Board of Trade and at the Treasury. He personified the rigours of post-war austerity and made a major contribution to the achievement of Indian independence.

In contrast to Attlee's marginality, Morrison had flourished at the party conference and there were subsequent rumours of a move to make him leader. Greenwood's Commons performances immediately before and during the early weeks of the war suggested for the first time that he too could be a credible leader, but Greenwood prevaricated and Attlee recovered both physically and politically. However, when Labour MPs met to elect their officers for the new session, Attlee faced opposition for the first time. Greenwood, Morrison and Dalton were all nominated. After Attlee had affirmed that he would not regard any challenge as evidence of disloyalty, all three withdrew. Subsequent events would guarantee Attlee's security for the duration of the war. Yet if Hitler's armies had not invaded Poland in September 1939, he would have led Labour to another decisive election defeat, which would have precipitated a serious leadership challenge.

Labour's support for the war was symbolised by an electoral truce, but the party remained outside the government. Suspicion of many ministers, not least Neville Chamberlain, ran deep. Early in May 1940 Attlee and his party secured a two-day Commons debate on the failure of a British military expedition to Norway. The debate provided a focus for the passionate expression of wider discontents about the government's performance. On the evidence of the first day's exchanges and after some hesitancy, the Labour leadership decided to force a vote. Forty Tory rebels backed by numerous abstentions inflicted fatal damage on Chamberlain's leadership, his majority plummeting from 250 to 81. Coalition was inevitable. In the subsequent negotiations Attlee was typically careful to act as the representative of his party. This commitment was underlined by the coincidence that Labour's annual conference was about to begin in Bournemouth. Labour's National Executive confirmed Attlee's assertion to

Chamberlain that the party would not serve under him but would do so under another prime minister. The party accepted office in a coalition headed by Winston Churchill; conference delegates overwhelmingly ratified this decision.

Attlee and Churchill rapidly settled ministerial appointments. Within a War Cabinet of five, Labour had two members, Attlee and Greenwood. Five more became ministers and a further seven took junior posts. Most significantly Ernest Bevin took leave from his union to become Minister of Labour. His initial response to the prospect of coalition had paralleled Attlee's. 'You helped to bring the other fellow down; if the Party did not take its share of responsibility, they would say we were not great citizens but cowards.'[7]

As the Coalition was being formed, German troops invaded the Low Countries and France. This *blitzkrieg*, within a few weeks, would mean the evacuation of the British Expeditionary Force from Dunkirk and the French government's abandonment of the struggle. Late in May, as British troops retreated to the coast the War Cabinet discussed the possibility that Mussolini, primed with suitable inducements, might act as an intermediary in the negotiation of an overall peace. One of Churchill's Conservative colleagues, the Foreign Secretary Lord Halifax, showed interest in the proposal, but Greenwood opposed any consideration and so, with characteristic brevity, did Attlee. In the Coalition's early months Churchill depended significantly on Labour support in government and in Parliament.

These weeks in May 1940 remade British politics for 40 years. Although the Conservative Party was not shattered by Chamberlain's removal, its established leadership was deeply discredited. Amongst the Tories the initiative passed to those who could claim, either accurately or mythically, a Churchillian pedigree in the foreign policy controversies of the 1930s.

Similarly Labour benefited from a rewriting of the recent past. Ambiguities and inconsistencies over rearmament could be buried. Such revisions were not restricted to politicians. In the summer of 1940 public opinion radicalised. The old gang had been electorally secure, but now they were condemned as incompetent and unpatriotic, a verdict captured in the title of that summer's celebrated polemic. They were 'guilty men'. The radicalisation was born in the context of threatened invasion and defeat. Expressed in the language of a people's war, it offered a progressive characterisation of the nation that drew upon varieties of liberalism and socialism. Military and foreign policy failures had broken the hegemony of Conservatism. One consequence was a radicalisation of opinion on economic and social issues that hitherto would have been unimaginable. For the Labour Party and for Attlee these developments offered opportunities and dangers.

Over the next five years, through 12 months of isolation to the alliances with the Soviet Union and the United States, from Dunkirk to the fall of Singapore, then El Alamein, Stalingrad and victory in Europe, one fact was evident. Labour members of the Coalition played crucial roles – Bevin, Morrison at the Home Office, and Cripps, still out of the party but recognised as on the Left, at Aircraft Production. Next to Churchill they did the vital jobs; but where in this role of honour was Attlee? His only departmental brief was at the Dominions Office from February 1942 until October 1943. Previously he had been Lord Privy Seal, subsequently he was Lord President. From February 1942 he was also designated Deputy Prime Minister. Apart from Churchill he was the only member of the War Cabinet throughout the Coalition's life. He sat on both the Defence Committee and the Lord President's Committee responsible for civil issues. His strengths became apparent to insiders. In Churchill's absence Cabinet business proceeded briskly. There were no monologues of marginal relevance. He was a conciliator who could be firm, not least with Churchill. In January 1945 he wrote at length to the Prime Minister detailing the latter's shortcomings in Cabinet. The overture captured Attlee's style. *I am stating the views I hold bluntly and frankly as I consider that it is my duty to do so.* Churchill's consequential wrath was not indulged by his closest political cronies. They backed Attlee; so did Churchill's wife. 'I admire Mr Attlee for having the courage to say what everyone is thinking.'[8]

Within the administration Attlee, as co-ordinator and facilitator, was ubiquitous. He reformed the committee system inherited from the previous government, enabling many issues to be resolved before they overloaded the Cabinet agenda. Such an indispensable figure, whatever his lack of flamboyance, acquired resources. This probably aided the inclusion of more Labour figures in the government. Bevin and Morrison joined Attlee in the War Cabinet, but Greenwood, a predictable failure, was dropped in 1942. In addition by the Coalition's final months 23 other posts had Labour incumbents.

Unostentatious achievements did nothing for Attlee's public reputation. Almost no-one thought of him as a possible Prime Minister. Within the Labour Party some still hoped for his replacement, usually by Morrison. However, one significant political relationship developed in the closeness and shared challenges of the War Cabinet. Prior to 1940 Attlee and Ernest Bevin had had limited contact. When Attlee became leader in 1935, his principal virtue for Bevin had been that he was not Herbert Morrison. Once in government, however, Bevin realised that Attlee did not conform to his stereotype of the unreliable politician. Rather he was straight and meant the little that he said. Attlee needed Bevin's support. Coalition achievements might restore Labour's credibility after the disaster of 1931, but many within the party felt frustrated.

As the threat of imminent invasion receded, Labour critics at all levels insisted that Labour ministers were doing little to advance progressive policies. Attlee had insisted from the beginning of the war that wartime challenges would necessitate socialist responses. But there seemed little evidence of such necessity. Attlee's style, Bevin's identity as trade unionist rather than partisan, and Morrison's taste for reasonable solutions all could suggest that coalition harmony mattered more than Labour's priorities.

Concern about ministerial missed opportunities was complemented by electoral anxiety. From spring 1942, the strength of popular radicalism was demonstrated in sensational by-election gains from Conservatives by both Left Independents and members of the new and socialist CommonWealth Party. Under the electoral truce local Labour parties were spectators; their members often supported the most radical candidate. Labour's National Agent, George Shepherd, saw serious dangers, not least concerning the party leader.

'It is not easy to work with a man in the afternoon in the Cabinet Room, and then in the evening appear to differ from him on the public platform … The Party must become distinctive again and Attlee must become a distinctive leader identified with the Party at least as much as he is with the Government.'[9]

Inevitably Attlee became a target of this resentment. Harold Laski, a critical voice on the National Executive

Committee, saw wartime radicalisation as offering a brief opportunity for significant change. He attacked Attlee privately and publicly for abandoning the party's principles. In response Attlee insisted that Laski ignored parliamentary arithmetic and was too optimistic about the outcome of an early election. Regular parliamentary critics were few and politically diverse. The most effective, Aneurin Bevan, employed the columns of *Tribune* to indict Attlee and his immediate colleagues.

Attlee's responses were often uninspiring but his leadership was never at risk. A loyal majority anchored in the trade unions dominated the party conference. Attlee and his ministerial colleagues commanded a majority on the National Executive. Parliamentary party meetings could be acrimonious as tensions between ministerial responsibility and party sentiments were exposed, but most Labour MPs, most of the time, remained loyal to the leadership. The most significant revolt came over the government's response to the Beveridge Report on social policy in February 1943. Within the War Cabinet Conservative ministers urged caution; their Labour colleagues advocated a positive response. The resulting decision avoided any commitment either positive or negative. The parliamentary party tabled an amendment for the Report's early implementation. This official party line was backed in the lobby by 97 Labour MPs. Labour ministers in effect became the rebels. Attlee's response was phlegmatic.

*I fear our people cannot ever understand when they've won. In fact they really prefer 'a glorious defeat' in the lobbies to a victory.*

ATTLEE

*So many of our fellows, good men not mischief makers, tend to use their hearts to the exclusion of their heads ... I fear our people cannot ever understand when they've won. In fact they really prefer 'a glorious defeat' in the lobbies to a victory. However, no doubt it will all blow over.*[10]

He was right. Beneath the conflicting loyalties Labour ministers remained attached to their distinctive programme. The necessities of wartime vindicated their advocacy of economic planning. Conservatives might block proposals for specific measures of public ownership but Labour's commitment to nationalisation remained firm, at least for specific industries. Labour began to incorporate an appreciation of Keynesian techniques of demand management into its economic outlook, but this complemented rather than replaced earlier attachments. After the Beveridge Report, Attlee and other senior Labour ministers pushed for progress on plans for reconstruction within the Coalition, but acknowledged that a return to partisan politics was inevitable.

In some respects the involvement of Attlee and his colleagues in the Coalition was an experience in the negotiation of consensus. They made agreements with Conservative colleagues on apparently divisive issues, they learnt much about the complexities of administration and the difficulties of reconciling visions with recalcitrant facts. There would be continuities of policy between war and post-war. But it is simplistic to claim that the basis for a subsequent consensus, however defined, lay in the ministerial experiences and togetherness of the Churchill Coalition.

Labour's leaving of the Coalition was messy. After the surrender of Germany early in May 1945, Attlee, Bevin and Dalton favoured the continuation of the Coalition until the defeat of Japan. Morrison insisted that party members would not accept this. No Labour politician had any awareness of the imminence of the American atomic bomb and therefore no expectation that Japanese surrender would be so rapid. Labour's leaders proposed October 1945 as the terminal date for the Coalition. Churchill responded by resigning as Coalition premier. The election was scheduled for 5 July. Attlee's Limehouse had been battered in the Blitz. More than half the pre-war electorate had moved out. The community that had made Attlee into a socialist had been transformed. *Instead of the packed masses of buildings there are wide open spaces with willow herbs growing on them.*[11]

The campaign soon destroyed any Coalition spirit. Churchill attacked the Labour Party in ridiculously extreme terms, insisting that his recent colleagues could achieve their objectives only though the employment of a 'Gestapo'. Attlee's low-key response was appropriate for an electorate that observers characterised as sober and thoughtful. The results, announced after a three-week interval to collect the service vote, were a sensation. Churchill, widely feted as the man who had won the war, was expected to emulate Lloyd George's electoral triumph in 1918. Instead Labour won 393 seats, over a hundred more than its previous best. Its overall majority was 146; its share of the vote was 47.8 per cent, up almost 10 per cent on 1935. Labour extended its dominance in previous areas of strength and spectacularly broke new ground. Its gains in London's suburbia, the Southeast and East Anglia were dramatic. Decades of Conservative dominance in Birmingham crumbled. The Members for Winchester and Wimbledon, King's Lynn and Cambridgeshire sat on the Labour benches.

*The King gave me his commission to form a Government. He always used to say that I looked very surprised, as indeed I certainly was at the extent of our success.*

ATTLEE

The Labour Party, despite the tension of the Coalition years, scooped a dual dividend – the credibility engendered by successful ministers and the legacy of wartime radicalism. The evidence had been there in opinion polls that politicians as yet ignored. Attlee's recollection of taking office was far removed from the dramatic images of his predecessor in May 1940. Mr Attlee had no sense of walking with destiny.

*The King gave me his commission to form a Government. He always used to say that I looked very surprised, as indeed I certainly was at the extent of our success. We went to a victory rally at Westminster Central Hall, where I announced that I had been charged with the task of forming a Government, looked in at a Fabian Society gathering and then returned to Stanmore after an exciting day.*[12]

A more representative recollection came from Hugh Dalton. 'We all knew that, within us, and because of us, and around us, something had suddenly changed.'[13]

# Part Two

THE LEADERSHIP

# Chapter 4: 'Annus Mirabilis'

Labour's 1945 election manifesto unapologetically proclaimed its political identity. 'The Labour Party is a Socialist Party and proud of it. Its ultimate purpose at home is the establishment of the Socialist Commonwealth of Great Britain.'[1] Many Labour supporters endorsed this socialism; for others, support for the party indicated a desire for jobs, decent housing and welfare flavoured with social egalitarianism. The instrument for such hopes was a party whose leaders, during the Coalition, had become accustomed to the mores of Whitehall. Socialised into administrative procedures and more broadly supportive of constitutional conventions, this socialist commitment was from the start expressed in practices that suggested continuity, none more so than in the sight of Attlee being driven to Buckingham Palace by his wife to accept the King's offer to form a government. The journey contrasted with the melodramatic rhythms of Churchillian rhetoric, yet its very lack of pretence somehow epitomised the change.

The journey to the Palace was accompanied by a private drama. Herbert Morrison as organiser and campaigner had had a triumphant election. As news of Labour gains flooded in on that memorable afternoon, he raised with Attlee his perennial objective, the party leadership, which now meant the premiership. He had the support of Cripps. The choice of a greatly expanded parliamentary party was uncertain. Attlee, on his own judgement and backed firmly by Ernest Bevin, responded rapidly to Churchill's resignation by accepting the King's commission, but Morrison and his acolytes continued to canvass for support among Labour MPs. The following day Morrison pursued the matter through a debatable interpretation of the party's agreed procedure for forming a government. He never had a chance. Attlee had led the party to a massive and unexpected triumph. Morrison's manoeuvres seemed self-serving, clumsy and irrelevant.

Attlee formed his first administration almost wholly from those who had sat in previous parliaments. He was well aware that his choice was in some areas limited. *Unfortunately the pre-election parliamentary Labour Party had been rather old, and there was not a great deal of ability while the new entry contained many men of high quality.*[2] He was keenly aware of the need to balance interests and identities, styles and talents, trade unionists and intellectuals. He showed no ideological partiality and did not discriminate against those who had colourful political records.

His first block of appointments covered his most senior colleagues. Greenwood was the least significant. His limitations were painfully obvious, but Attlee was aware of his popularity, loyalty and seniority within the party. Given a non-departmental post, he served until removed in an extensive reshuffle in October 1947. Greenwood's surviving reputation owed much to sentiment, but other senior colleagues remained powerful figures in their own right and the effectiveness of Attlee's government would depend heavily on his relationships with them, and their relationships with one another.

Morrison's frustrated ambition was assuaged by responsibilities that were both prestigious and exacting. The title Deputy Prime Minister was perhaps a consolation prize.

As overlord of economic planning he became the target of criticism from some colleagues, but as Leader of the Commons he provided the organising and bargaining skills, a blend of the consensual and the partisan, and the élan that facilitated the passage of an ambitious legislative programme. His concern with discipline was tempered by an appreciation that the large and diverse parliamentary party had to be handled sympathetically. His relationship with Attlee could never be close, but Morrison provided skills essential to the government's effectiveness.

Hugh Dalton (Eton and King's) might be expected to have much in common with Attlee, but whereas Attlee was discreet, self-effacing and private, Dalton was loud, extroverted and crudely conspiratorial. Like Morrison he could never quite work out why Attlee had become and remained leader. As Attlee's Chancellor of the Exchequer, he, more than any minister, proclaimed the government's early optimism, but this ebullience was destroyed by the economic turmoil of 1947. A venial disclosure of budget proposals to a journalist forced his resignation. Attlee offered no protection. His subsequent verdict that Dalton had made a great mistake was an uncharacteristic exaggeration. He might well have welcomed the chance to marginalise an inveterate plotter who had become associated with economic crisis. Dalton's rapid return to the Cabinet did not mean a political resurrection.

Cripps, his successor as Chancellor, had not been an orthodox party figure. Close to Attlee after 1931, his unpredictable radicalism and eventual expulsion in 1939 had preceded a politically good war. His concern for efficiency had led to brief and fanciful speculation that he might replace Churchill. His ministerial record and late re-entry into the Labour Party meant that he would be a significant figure in the government. An industrious beginning at the Board of Trade was punctuated by three months in 1946 as the dominant figure in a three-man Cabinet mission to India. Cripps' status grew as Dalton's declined. As Chancellor from November 1947, he represented a demanding and in many respects effective strategy for economic recovery. A personification of austerity and probity, he harmonised with Attlee's own style. By 1949, he rivalled Morrison as the dominant personality on the home front.

Attlee's dealings with these key figures were correct, reasoned and rather formal. He had more affection for the one trade unionist within this senior group. *My relationship with Ernest Bevin was the deepest of my political life. I was very fond of him and I understand that he was very fond of me.*[3] Their contrasting lives encapsulated the harsh inequalities of late Victorian Britain. In contrast to the security of Putney, Bevin was illegitimate, born into rural poverty in 1881, orphaned and briefly a farm worker before being pitchforked onto the Bristol labour market. In 1910, as Attlee was drilling East End youths, Bevin was organising Bristol carters into the Dockers' Union. As architect of the post-war Transport and General Workers' Union he constructed a base for industrial and political influence. His forceful response to the 1931 crisis, his blend of insight and idiosyncrasy and his strength of character had made him the dominant trade union leader of the 1930s.

In Bevin's eyes Attlee was the antithesis of Morrison. He did not fit the stereotype of an unreliable and devious politician. Bevin's support was also a basic matter of loyalty to a party leader who was sensitive to trade union concerns. For Attlee, Bevin, his creativity unhampered by much formal

*My relationship with Ernest Bevin was the deepest of my political life. I was very fond of him and I understand that he was very fond of me.*

ATTLEE

education, perhaps recalled the boys that he had met in the East End. Ernest Bevin's working class, not that of the respectable craftsmen, was the working class that had brought him to socialism. Both men understood how workers with no conventional skill to sell were particularly vulnerable to the arbitrary whims of the employers. Solidarity was essential but elusive. The Transport and General and Workers' and the Stepney Labour Party were both responses to this challenge. Although Attlee's initial Cabinet contained several trade unionists, Bevin alone was a political heavyweight who could claim to speak for a broad trade union constituency as opposed to a specific occupational interest. Memories of 1931 recalled the grim consequences for the labour movement when politicians and trade unionists went from misunderstanding to mistrust, division and disaster. Arthur Henderson in 1931 had backed the TUC in the MacDonald Cabinet. Bevin took this role under Attlee. He was 'the keeper of the cloth cap'.

Bevin's appointment as Foreign Secretary was a surprise, not least to himself. He had expected and preferred the Treasury, whereas Dalton had anticipated the Foreign Office. Attlee's initial thoughts favoured that outcome, but he rapidly reversed his assessment. Subsequent speculation about the reasons has included the suggestion of Royal influence. However Attlee's own explanation included the need for internal harmony. *Bevin and Morrison must be kept apart. I was not really convinced that Dalton's temperament really fitted him for the Foreign Office ... as Chancellor ... Bevin would have been certain to have got into controversy with Morrison.*[4]

Several appointments were self-evident. Tom Williams, a Yorkshire miners' member, had made himself into Labour's agricultural expert after 1931. He had served in the Department throughout the Coalition and now took the senior post. A V Alexander, once considered a possible leader, went to the Admiralty, the post he had held in 1929, and again in 1940. However, sometimes expectations based on expertise proved misleading. Chuter Ede, once a teacher, had served at Education throughout the Coalition and had been heavily involved in the passing of the 1944 Education Act. He was a firm supporter of Attlee. Ellen Wilkinson had acquired a perhaps exaggerated pre-war reputation as a rebel. She was personally very close to Morrison and had been heavily involved in his periodic manoeuvres for the leadership. For Attlee the last consideration was characteristically irrelevant.

*The obvious choice for education would have been Chuter Ede, but I needed a man of great wisdom, judgement and firmness of character for the Home Office. I wanted a woman in the Cabinet and Ellen Wilkinson who had learnt responsibility as undersecretary in the Ministry of Home Security during the war, was very well qualified.*[5]

After she died in February 1947 no other woman was ever appointed to an Attlee Cabinet. Wilkinson's successor was George Tomlinson, a Lancastrian textile trade unionist whose folksy stories were prized by Attlee as encapsulating working-class wisdom, an antidote to the speculations of more cerebral colleagues. Attlee had a similar appreciation of a much more influential figure, the Chief Whip William Whiteley. He symbolised the reliably loyal Labour politics of the Durham coalfield. *A dignified presence ... a fine character ... absolutely just, he was firm yet conciliatory.*[6] Whiteley's influence was largely private. So was that of Lord Addison. Admired by Attlee as MacDonald's Minister of Agriculture, he now led the small Labour contingent in the House of Lords. His political experience went back to Edwardian Progressive Liberalism. He became one of Attlee's few confidantes.

A photograph of Attlee's initial Cabinet shows a gallery of obviously respectable and sober men. There are two exceptions. At the far right sits Ellen Wilkinson. And at the extreme left of the second row stands a man clearly younger than his colleagues and somehow separate, not a thorough member of this club. Aneurin Bevan (1897–1960) was Attlee's most surprising Cabinet appointment. Since his entry to Parliament in 1929 Bevan had collaborated with Mosley until the latter quit the party, then campaigned for a Popular Front and been expelled along with Cripps, and had attacked party and TUC leaders with a vigour restrained only by a belief that Labour was the only political instrument available to the British working class. During the war he had been one of Churchill's most effective and passionate critics. Attlee felt that this critic could be creative. *At Health took chance, Bevan had the ability but might not have judgment – ability as administrator yet to be displayed.*[7]

*At Health took chance, Bevan had the ability but might not have judgment – ability as administrator yet to be displayed.*

ATTLEE

Labour's long-standing commitments to the pubic ownership of coal, gas and electricity made the Ministry of Fuel and Power a significant and potentially sensitive appointment. In this case Attlee's choice proved less happy. Emmanuel Shinwell, an acerbic critic of the wartime Coalition, seemed to him the best available. His style was vigorous. He had served at the Mines Department in the pre-war Labour governments.

Inevitably failure, ill health, age and death brought changes. The first major reshuffle in October 1947 brought the first 1945 entrant, Harold Wilson, into the Cabinet. Generational change came slowly, however. Attlee acquired, at least in retrospect, a reputation as a good butcher who did not hesitate to remove the incompetent. Yet some ministers felt that he sometimes moved too slowly and too cautiously. Against such criticisms are the anecdotes about brief encounters between Attlee and ministers unsuspecting of their imminent demise. Such brevity could be an expression of toughness or a strategy by which a shy man coped with the uncongenial.

Attlee's own notes provide mixed evidence. Individuals' shortcomings are chronicled along with their consequential fates. Fred Bellenger rose to be Secretary of State for War in October 1946, but lasted barely a year. *On bad advice I made Bellenger who had done well as under sec to be of S of S War. He was not up to the position and had to go.*[8] Bellenger's roots in the party were notably shallow. In contrast Phillip Noel Baker had been a prominent party figure on international affairs since the 1920s. Despite his qualities Attlee found his ministerial record disappointing. Entering the Cabinet at Commonwealth Relations in October 1947 he *did not inspire much confidence, his judgement was poor. He was talkative but not illuminating in Cabinet.*[9] Yet Attlee retained him in the Cabinet, even shifting him after a hard tussle to the unfamiliar territory of Fuel and Power. Status in the wider party, deserved or not, could not be ignored.

Leading this diverse and talented team was a challenge. The Cabinet included men with strong opinions and significant support within both the party and the wider labour movement. Attlee's management of Cabinet meetings was a national version of his Stepney mayoralty. He vetoed irrelevant and unfocused contributions, except for Bevin who was permitted monologues that combined reminiscence, egoism and illumination. Attlee could be sharply critical of ministers who had not mastered their briefs, and his praise was rare and sparse. As chair he rarely attempted to lead discussion, preferring to sum up the balance of an argument. This style could facilitate decisions by a potentially disputatious group, but at critical moments when opinion was sharply divided or ministers were uncertain it could suggest a lack of direction.

Attlee's first government enjoyed the benefit of a large parliamentary majority and initially of an uncertain and sometimes demoralised Opposition. Even as Conservative combativeness revived in the wake of economic difficulties, Labour MPs remained broadly optimistic about the government's performance and about electoral prospects. This parliamentary party was diverse. There were contrasts of generation, class, education, occupation, region and nation. Sir Charles Edwards of the South Wales Miners, born in 1867, had represented Bedwelty since 1918. Albert Stubbs, an organiser of agricultural workers had first contested Cambridgeshire in 1918; in 1945 he won there by 44 votes. In contrast to such veterans, Major Woodrow Wyatt, born 1920, Oxford-educated and mentioned in despatches, stood briefly on the left of the party; he would later become a devotee of Margaret Thatcher. Trade union loyalists sat alongside ethical socialists weaned on the culture of the ILP, a garrulous exponent of the idiosyncratic Social Credit doctrine, admirers of the Soviet Union and members who brought a kaleidoscope of industrial and military experiences to debate. There were only 21 women. Even for them issues of sexual equality were rarely a priority. For most members, their formative experiences were the economic and international crises of the inter-war years, and then the radical expectations unleashed in Britain and elsewhere since 1939. Diversity proved compatible with cohesion. Despite economic constraints and crises there was full employment and an impressive expansion of welfare. Notwithstanding housing shortages and a broader climate of austerity, this record cemented the loyalty of backbenchers. Never before had a party programme so prefigured a government's legislation.

Many Labour MPs found Attlee a remote figure. Their

deference and uncertainty, his shyness and lack of social conversation guaranteed this. He was not convivial even amongst those who knew him better. There was often a terse formality. His expeditions into Commons' bars could end relaxed discussion in favour of stilted exchanges. Such distance might have been a source of strength. At critical moments Attlee's low-key approach could deflect discontent.

Harmony on the home front was not complemented initially by consensus on international affairs. For at least two years there was significant criticism of government policy. Many MPs had cherished the hope of a socialist foreign policy. Opacity of content did not diminish its emotional appeal. Some were inspired by the ethics of the ILP, some by support for the Soviet Union, many by a general distaste for power politics. But it rapidly became apparent that government international policy had strong continuities with its Coalition predecessor.

> One of the 21 Labour women of 1945 was Barbara Castle (1910–2003). Prominent on the left and a passionate supporter of Aneurin Bevan, she joined the Wilson government in 1964 initially in 1964 as Minister of Overseas Development and the following year entered the Cabinet at Transport. From 1968 she was Secretary of State for Employment and Productivity. Her white paper *In Place of Strife* proposed legal regulation of industrial relations and brought her into conflict with the trade unions. Lack of Cabinet support meant her abandonment of the proposals. In the 1974 Wilson administration she was Secretary of State for Social Services but did not retain office in the Callaghan premiership.

Ernest Bevin's robust criticism of the Soviet Union appalled some backbenchers and troubled many more. However, Bevin had loyal, if often silent, supporters on the backbenches, and was allowed much freedom by senior colleagues.

In November 1946, with Bevin absent in New York, Attlee

defended the government's foreign policy in the Commons against extensive backbench criticism. His defence came in general and sometimes 'ad hominem' terms. *The attacks I have seen made on the foreign secretary, are made often by people whose services in the cause of labour and Socialism are as dust in the balance compared with his.*[10] Whatever the emerging pattern of international relations, the government had significant ideological differences with the United States. *They hold a capitalist philosophy which we do not accept. Rather in matters of economic planning we agree with Soviet Russia.*[11] On democracy the attachment was reversed. But Attlee emphasised that ideology offered only a limited guide to international affairs, an admonition similar to his assessment of Indian complexities at the time of the Simon Commission.

Despite this Prime Ministerial intervention, the critics were numerous. About 120 Labour backbencher abstained at the end of the debate, but the deepening Cold War gradually eroded their numbers. Only a handful were resolutely pro-Soviet, while many hoped for a democratic socialist European alternative to Russian and American models. By early 1948 this prospect was clearly dead. Most Labour backbenchers ultimately accepted the polarities of the Cold War. Some did so zealously but many had regrets. For the time being harmony in the parliamentary party increased.

Even when a backbench revolt produced a modification in government policy, Attlee was phlegmatic. In spring 1947 legislation for the continuation of military service provoked a sizeable revolt in the lobbies and a consequential cut in the proposed length of service from 18 months to 12. Attlee seemed at ease with an explanation based on stereotypes, not ideological difference. *I am not unduly worried over the conscription debate. The old traditional ILP sentiments naturally prevailed with some of our senior members while the Welsh voted strongly against us. I think that they have too great a fear of Welsh nationalism. The remainder were mostly young people who have not yet settled down.*[12]

Ministerial ascendancy over backbenchers was matched by control of the party in the country. A critical left existed; its sentiments were articulated at party conferences by constituency activists and some trade union delegates. Even when such criticisms struck a chord they were rejected. The record of Attlee and his colleagues was underwritten consistently. An alliance of major trade unions was central to this predictability. The two large general unions, the Transport Workers' and the monolithically right-wing General and Municipal Workers combined with the National Union of Mineworkers to produce almost decisive backing for the government. The politics of some other unions, including the Engineers and Railwaymen, were less predictable. One dominant emotion was loyalty to the first majority Labour government. Moreover as international politics became captured increasingly in Cold War images, so trade union politics became expressed more and more through the Communist–anti-Communist factionalism that had characterised several unions since the 1920s. In this climate criticisms of government policy need not be discussed on their merits, but could simply be dismissed as Communist-inspired.

Within this wider political world Attlee's was a minor voice. His conference set-pieces could seem like the annual report of a headmaster on speech day. In contrast the star turns were Bevin, earthy realism and loyalty; Bevan, socialist passion and creativity; Cripps, austere morality; and Morrison the chirpy and accomplished professional. A network of bargains ensured trade union acquiescence in government policies. Attlee's security rested on complex practices and their attendant attitudes that extended far beyond the parliamentary party. The effectiveness of these supportive networks rarely depended on his direct interventions. The only credible threat to his position might come from immediate colleagues – a coup, not a peasants' revolt.

Political security was complemented by a broader comfort in the job. Attlee seems not to have felt overwhelmed by his responsibilities. He sought to address and hopefully solve problems on the basis of consensus, first within the government, then within the labour movement, and finally and perhaps over-optimistically within wider society. Such optimism reflected how his commitment to socialism cohabited with social conservatism. He had no scepticism about most constitutional conventions nor about the numerous assumptions expectations and taboos that characterised the institutions of the British state. He was at ease with the ceremonial aspects of his responsibilities. His enthusiasms were evident at Lords and Wimbledon. He and his impeccably middle-class family enjoyed Chequers and Royal hospitality. Only on policy did Attlee show any inclination to break with the past.

Attlee's collegial style often meant that he made no distinctive impact on government policy. He expressed or helped to construct an agreed Cabinet position which was informed typically by the priorities, judgements and prejudices of dominant and relevant department ministers. This style of leadership could falter when key colleagues were divided or unsure of a solution. Such difficulties usually arose not over the implementation of the agreed programme, but over unexpected and critical developments where the knowledge of ministers and the precepts of party offered little guidance.

Such a crisis confronted ministers within weeks of taking office. The British war effort had meant the loss of about one-quarter of the national wealth. The government faced massive overseas indebtedness, a cut in overseas income due to the sale of assets and a shrunken export trade, an escalating bill for essential imports and a trebling of the national debt. Wartime levels of consumption had depended on Lend-Lease from the United States. Keynes warned ministers of a financial Dunkirk. He insisted that a bearable standard of living and any British claim to great-power status necessitated long-term aid of around $5 billion from the US. Such a prospect was a discordant commentary on popular hopes for economic and social improvement. On 21 August 1945, just six days after the surrender of Japan, the American government abruptly terminated Lend-Lease, an act characterised by some as an American attempt to puncture socialist dreams. Attlee was shocked but typically undramatic.

*We had hoped that the sudden cessation of this great mutual effort … would not have been effected without consultation and prior discussion … the sudden cessation of a support on which our war organisation has so largely depended, puts us in a very serious financial position.*[13]

Keynes headed a delegation to Washington, hoping initially for a grant or an interest-free loan. Cultures and expectations collided. The Americans held all the cards. Dalton recalled: 'We retreated slowly and with a bad grace and with increasing irritation from a free gift to an interest-free loan and from this again to a loan bearing interest; from a larger to a smaller total of aid; and from the prospect of loose strings, some of which would only be general declarations of intention, to the most unwilling acceptance of strings so tight that they might strangle our trade and indeed our own economic life.'[14] Ernest Bevin, midway through the negotiations, expressed the realism of the seasoned trade union negotiator. 'I hate the idea of getting under US control. But situation I'm faced with is – can you carry thro' British people for next 3 years on lower rations. I believe our bluff is called … We are in Shylock's hands.'[15]

By early December all was settled. The loan would be for $3.75 billion at 2 per cent interest to be repaid in 50 annual instalments from 1951. From the end of 1946 British trade controls should not discriminate against the United States. Britain must make a commitment to joint Anglo-American proposals for multilateral trade. Sterling must be convertible into dollars and other currencies. The due date for convertibility would be one year after Congressional approval of the loan, in the event 15 July 1947.

Attlee had visited Washington in November 1945. His chief concern had been to discuss atomic energy policy with President Truman. His address to Congress emphasising Labour's commitment to both democracy and socialism was typically straightforward, but might have confirmed some in their prejudices about likely British misuse of American money. Within the Cabinet, Dalton, Bevin, Morrison and Cripps reluctantly accepted the necessity for a loan. When the Cabinet discussed a draft agreement on 29 November, the only overt opposition came from Shinwell and Aneurin Bevan. Shinwell felt that the conditions were incompatible with a planned economy, while Bevan felt that more firmness should be shown towards the Americans. Attlee simply summarised the discussion. The preponderant view was clearly to proceed on the basis of the draft proposals. When the final terms were discussed on 5 December, only Shinwell voiced opposition, but the Cabinet agreed without any formal dissent. The Agreement was decisively ratified in the Commons. Twenty-three Labour members opposed it; the Conservatives were deeply divided. The Cabinet had remained united on the basis that the loan was preferable to the credible alternatives and was essential for progress on

Labour's social programme. Senior Labour ministers within the Coalition, with the exception of Bevin, had been sympathetic to American proposals for trade liberalisation as a central element in the reconstruction of the international economy. However, the episode had given Labour ministers a sharp lesson in the realities of Anglo-American relations.

The months that followed the negotiation of the loan produced a stream of legislation, most notably on welfare provision and public ownership. The South Wales Miners' Member, James Griffiths, piloted through a comprehensive National Insurance Bill without serious opposition. This consolidated all forms of insurance on a principle of universality. A similar lack of controversy attended the extension of public ownership to civil aviation and cable and wireless. Public ownership of the Bank of England recalled in Labour legend the trauma of 1931. For many within the labour movement, coal nationalisation seemed the termination of a history of insecurity, poor wages and conditions, broken promises and conflict. The ceremonies at pitheads on New Year's Day 1947 to mark the demise of the coalowners symbolised the hopes invested by miners in Attlee's government.

This triumphal progress justified Dalton's recollection of 1946 as Labour's 'Annus mirabilis'. It demonstrated Attlee's preference for competent ministers to get on with their departmental agendas. This ability was particularly evident in the case of his most unexpected appointment. Aneurin Bevan was allowed scope to extend and amend the proposals for a National Health Service that had developed under the Coalition. When his own proposals came to Cabinet in October and December 1945, one element proved contentious. Voluntary and municipal hospitals were to be brought together under regional boards, directly responsible to the minister. This proposal for the nationalisation of hospitals was attacked by Morrison as an erosion of local democracy. Criticism also came from Chuter Ede and Alexander. Dalton had financial anxieties. However, Bevan had the support of Addison, not just Attlee's confidante but also a one-time celebrated anatomist. Crucially Attlee strongly steered the Cabinet in Bevan's favour. By March 1946, a Bill had been introduced. Over the next two years, the government won a vital trial of strength against an obdurate British Medical Association cheered on by revitalised Tories. At a critical moment Attlee had acted decisively and subsequently backed his minister against sometime venomous critics. The outcome was arguably the government's most outstanding achievement. Yet the initial disagreement left a poisonous residue. Morrison had long been suspicious of Bevan. Perhaps this Cabinet victory, achieved with Attlee's support, fuelled Morrison's later criticisms of Bevan's stewardship of the Health Service.

Beyond any specific intervention was Attlee's contribution to the style of his administration. Labour sought to strengthen the communal sentiments of the 'People's War', not least through a discourse of fair shares. The socially useful were to be admired, the parasitic should be condemned. This morality linked readily to the ethical socialism that Attlee had imbibed and articulated in Limehouse. It also connected with the language of radicalism employed by Lloyd George in his Edwardian assaults on reactionary peers. The power of such language, always perhaps less effective than its advocates believed, diminished as the omnipresence of war gave way to peacetime preoccupations. In particular fair shares through rationing became a subject of political controversy. In July 1946 bread rationing was introduced, which had never been imposed during the war. The following day Labour faced a by-election at Bexley in suburban Kent. Its majority fell by almost 10,000 with a swing to the Conservatives of over 11 per cent. Bexley was typical of several constituencies that Labour had won for the first time a year earlier. The warning was clear. Whatever the welfare and other legislative achievements of the government, for at least some electors the level and the quality of consumption really mattered. Perhaps for many voters in established Labour communities comparisons with inter-war experiences might work to the government's advantage. Elsewhere they might not. The rhetoric of community and public service might mask significant social divisions.

Social and political divisions on domestic questions cohabited with a contrasting alignment on international affairs. There the continuities with Coalition priorities and assumptions were evident and there was frequent agreement between Government and Opposition leaderships. Early post-war controversy was within the Labour Party as some clung to a belief in a socialist foreign policy in the face of Bevin's robust defence of a conventionally-defined national interest, typically articulated against the demands and resistance of the Soviet Union. How far Bevin was a significant architect of British policy, how far he endorsed with personalised ornamentation established Foreign Office views about Soviet beliefs and priorities and British interests, remains controversial. What is undeniable is that Bevin's policy was endorsed in public by his Cabinet colleagues, most symbolically in Attlee's Commons defence in November 1946. In Cabinet there was support for Bevin's actions. Bevin's forceful character and the close relationship between him and Attlee could suggest that he was given a free hand. Attlee's retrospective judgement supported this assessment. *Foreign affairs are the province of the foreign secretary. It is in my view a mistake for the Prime Minister to intervene personally except in the most exceptional circumstances. There's a lot in the proverb. 'If you've got a good dog don't bark yourself'.*[16]

The reality was more complicated, at least for the first 18 months of the Labour government. Attlee's pre-war views on the Soviet Union and Communism could be less antagonistic than some of his colleagues. Certainly his ethical socialism owed nothing to Marxism. Yet the East End left in the 1920s had involved frequent collaboration between Labour and Communist, so much so that the Mile End, Whitechapel and Bethnal Green Labour organisations were purged in the more exclusive climate of 1926–7. Attlee's position is unclear but it seems improbable that he was wholly comfortable with this hard line. When Attlee visited the Soviet Union in 1936, his response was often positive, not least to the ordered enjoyment of Moscow's Park of Rest and Culture. He was inevitably aware of the cult of Stalin, but seemingly oblivious to the burgeoning terror. Rather he considered that *the ordinary citizen supports the existing rulers because he believes they are carrying out a programme which is for his good, and which he himself desires.*[17] More broadly Attlee's eminence within the Labour Party had entailed frequent interventions on international affairs. He had insisted that a socialist government would make a distinctive contribution. *There is a deep difference of opinion between the Labour Party and the capitalist parties on foreign as well as home policy, because the two cannot be separated. The foreign policy of a Government is the reflection of its internal policy.*[18]

Inevitably Attlee's involvement at the highest level within the Churchill Coalition meant that he encountered Foreign Office views about the likely challenges in post-war Europe. On most issues, including sensitivity about Soviet ambitions, Attlee was in agreement with the Coalition Foreign Secretary

Anthony Eden. When, following the liberation of Greece, British troops were used against the Communist-led resistance movement Attlee stood firmly with his ministerial colleagues. In April 1945 he accompanied Eden to the founding conference of the United Nations in San Francisco. Between the election and the counting of the votes he travelled to Potsdam with Churchill and Eden where he was a largely silent observer of discussions with President Truman and Stalin. When Attlee and Bevin left the post-election celebrations for further Potsdam discussions, continuity on foreign policy, not socialist innovation, was endorsed by Labour's most senior figures.

However the Coalition years had also influenced Attlee in a more heterodox direction. He had become sceptical about Britain's ability to fully maintain itself as a major power. In particular he focussed on the Middle East where extensive British commitments were the product of a conception of imperial defence rendered anachronistic by the rise of air power. With Labour's electoral victory, Attlee's heterodoxy suddenly became much more significant. However, Bevin's performance at Potsdam, accompanied by the taciturn Attlee, rapidly reassured the Permanent Secretary at the Foreign Office, Sir Alexander Cadogan. 'Bevin I think will do well. He knows a great deal, is prepared to read any amount, seems to take in what he does read and is capable of making up his own mind about sticking up for his (or our) point of view against anyone. I think he's the best we could have had.'[19] His status within the labour movement could be turned to good account. 'He's the heavyweight of the Cabinet and will get his own way with them so, if he can be put on the right line, that may be all right.'[20]

Throughout 1946 there was no public evidence of any Prime Ministerial scepticism about any aspect of his own administration's foreign policy. His defence against backbench critics in the November debate cast doubt on any easy reliance on socialist principles. *The fundamental misconception here is of the nature and problem of international relations ... In foreign affairs however perfect our policy it can be carried out only in conjunction with other nations ... Geography of course is not altered by a general election.*[21]

*In foreign affairs however perfect our policy it can be carried out only in conjunction with other nations ... Geography of course is not altered by a general election.*

ATTLEE

A few weeks previously speaking at the Trades Union Congress, he had been briefed for a speech that would be critical of the Soviet Union. He attacked misrepresentation from *members of the Communist party their dupes and fellow travellers*, and poured scorn on their double standards. *If in any part of the world, the Communist Party by no matter what means is in power, that is democracy. If anywhere the Communists fail, then however fair the conditions, it is Fascism.*[22] Ernest Bevin could not have said it better.

Within the Cabinet Attlee gave firm backing to his Foreign Secretary, but throughout 1946 their private exchanges could be more discordant. Contrary to the arguments of Bevin, the Foreign Office and the Chiefs of Staff, Attlee opposed any acquisition of former Italian colonies, especially Cyrenacia. In a characteristic Attlee phrase they were *deficit areas* and would be one more burden on a hard-pressed Treasury. Moreover, demands for self-government would soon arise. Such problems should be avoided, not least because in Attlee's view the Middle East should no longer be a central strategic concern. Attlee and Bevin discussed these questions at Chequers on 27 December 1946. A few days later on 5 January 1947 Attlee produced a seven-page memorandum.

Entitled *Near Eastern Policy*, this was the final flowering of his heterodoxy.

Attlee began by summarising the position of the Chiefs of Staff. Britain was vulnerable to attack by long-range weapons; a credible deterrent was essential. The Soviet Union was the only plausible enemy; the Middle East was the only realistic location for a deterrent force. British bases would also protect the oil supply and guarantee the security of the Mediterranean. Support should be given to several Middle Eastern states, and the Soviet Union should be denied any foothold in the region. In Attlee's judgement this strategy would have destabilising consequences. The Russians would perceive not deterrence but preparation for offensive action, and subsequent Russian countermeasures would heighten tensions. Western Europe, its states weakened by war, was vulnerable. *Resistance will only be possible after a period of some years in which the economic revival of Europe has made good progress and has been accompanied by a falling off in the attraction which Communism offers to countries in a state of economic depression ... A period of peace will permit the strengthening of western conceptions of democracy.* His hope for stability in Western Europe was complemented by optimism about the possibility of change in the outlook of the Soviet regime. *The more international tension relaxes the less possible will it be to maintain in the USSR the war mentality and war economy that has persisted since the revolution. The best hope of enduring peace lies in a change in the character of the regime in the USSR.* At least resistance in Western Europe involved the politically congenial. In the Middle East the Chiefs of Staff line meant alliances with states that were weak militarily, economically and demographically – and which were politically disreputable. *There is a small class of wealthy and corrupt people at the top and a mass of poverty stricken land workers at the bottom. Their Governments are essentially reactionary*

*...We shall constantly appear to be supporting vested interests and reaction against reform and revolution in the interests of the poor.* The position of the Chiefs of Staff was characterised as a counsel of despair, only to be resorted to as a final option. Rather the way forward must be to attempt serious negotiations with the Russians on specific points of difference. Feasibility depended on basic uncertainties – the commitment or otherwise of the Soviet Union to world revolution, the possibility of convincing the USSR that *we have no offensive intentions against her*, the prospect of a change in the Russian outlook and an assessment of whether the Soviet Union could be persuaded that war with the United States was not inevitable.[23]

Attlee's exposition did not proclaim a socialist foreign policy, but presented a measured argument for flexible and empathetic diplomacy, a synthesis of ethical and pragmatic politics, underpinned by a thorough awareness of British economic weakness. Foreign Office opinion was unyielding. Communism was an aggressive ideology. The Soviet Union was an expansionary power. Flexibility would be interpreted as weakness with the consequence that a demoralised Western Europe would become a prey to destabilisation, while elsewhere Communist objectives would be pursued under convenient fig leaves such as anti-colonialism. Negotiation, as proposed by Attlee, was a non-runner.

Bevin replied to Attlee on 9 January 1947, or rather signed a document that presented the Foreign Office orthodoxy. He stigmatised Attlee's position as a reversal of the policy that he had pursued in the Middle East with Cabinet agreement. Any British retrenchment in the region would create a situation captured in that favourite Foreign Office metaphor, a vacuum, that would be gratefully occupied by the Soviet Union. Attlee's strategy would repeat the folly of Munich, an abuse of history that would have many imitators. 'A surrender of the type you suggest would only encourage the Russian leaders to believe that they could get there ... without war and would lead them into the same error that Hitler made of thinking that he could get away with anything by bluff and bullying ... It would be Munich all over again.' The questions to which Attlee wished to find answers were already settled for Bevin and his officials. 'The present rulers of Russia are committed to the belief that there is a natural conflict between the capitalist and the communist worlds. They also believe that they have a mission to work for a communist world.'[24] Such certainty ignored the impact of Nazi aggression on Russian resources and their sense of security.

The dispute was settled, not by the merits of arguments but by the resources commanded by the contestants. Also on 9 January Attlee met with Bevin and with A V Alexander, a faithful advocate of military orthodoxy. No officials were present and no minutes were taken. Bevin's own account to a senior official indicated that Attlee, despite voicing continuing concerns, had conceded his case. A further discussion with the Chiefs of Staff present underlined this assessment. In part the outcome reflected Attlee's isolation in a private battle in which he was opposed by two major departments, the Foreign Office and Defence. Little of the controversy percolated beyond the principals. Certainly Dalton as Chancellor had been aware of Attlee's scepticism about Middle East strategy in the spring of 1946, and, given his search for expenditure cuts, had been sympathetic, but in January 1947 Dalton was not involved. What mattered politically was Attlee's relationship with Bevin. Although this disagreement raised basic questions about Soviet intentions, its focus was very specific. Attlee and Bevin agreed on most foreign policy issues. Attlee's own position depended significantly on Bevin's support. There were compelling reasons to acquiesce.

Whether the rejection of Attlee's proposals represented a lost opportunity raises complex questions about the intentions of the principal actors. The episode also poses the question of the extent of choice available to a British government. Attlee had suggested significant amendments in the name of realism to British Great Power expectations. It is questionable how far such expectations could have been deflated by any elected government in the aftermath of military victory. Attlee's initiative was buried both by the intensification of the Cold War and in the privacy of Whitehall.

Only a few ministers knew of the most dramatic manifestation of British great power expectations. During the war, the American, British and Canadian governments had pooled expertise for the production of an atomic weapon. The practice had been formalised in the Quebec Agreement of 1943. Attlee's visit to Washington in November 1945 had produced agreement to continue technical collaboration, but British expectations were frustrated. The passing of the MacMahon Act in August 1946 prohibited American co-operation on nuclear research with any other state. The episode characterised the uncertainties of Anglo-American relations in the two years after the defeat of Germany. From late 1945, a secret Cabinet committee, GEN75, had considered atomic energy. Its membership was restricted to the most senior ministers, plus John Wilmot, the Minister of Supply. In October 1946 the committee assessed the options in the light of the MacMahon Act. A belief that maintenance of Britain's international status necessitated continuing research in the field was countered by an admonition about scarce economic resources. The specific issue of a British atomic bomb was not mentioned. The decisive moment came in January 1947 just as Attlee was acquiescing in the established Middle East policy. The two economic ministers, Dalton and

Cripps, were not involved. A smaller group – Attlee, Bevin, Morrison, Addison and Wilmot – were reconstituted as a new committee, GEN163. They agreed to go ahead with the secret construction of a British atomic bomb. Other ministers were not informed. A strong concern with international credibility was complemented by anxiety that the American presidential election in 1948 might produce a more isolationist Republican administration. These few Labour ministers, and doubtless most of their unaware colleagues, were unable to acquiesce in an American monopoly. Possession of an independent British bomb would bring influence, not least in Washington. This argument, articulated by Bevin, was endorsed by Attlee. This secret decision would leave a thoroughly divisive legacy for future generations of Labour politicians.

Several within the Labour Party went along reluctantly with their government's bipartisanship in international affairs, but in contrast all were enthusiastic about its record on India. Labour's 1945 election manifesto had included a vague commitment to 'the advancement of India to responsible self-government'.[25] Little more than two years later, on 15 August 1947, the British quit India. Subsequent Labour characterisations claimed that the election of a Labour government had made a decisive difference. Churchill's pre-war record on India suggested that under his premiership such a change would have been unimaginable. Many commentators have placed particular emphasis on Attlee's role. One biographer has insisted that 'it was his own most important contribution to the history of his time, and the role he played in bringing it about surpassed that of any of his colleagues'.[26] The reality was more complex.

Attlee's pre-war involvement in Indian affairs had been episodic – essentially the Simon Commission and the debate leading up to the 1935 Act. In each case he had supported

# Attlee and Europe

Attlee appeared in style and pursuits a quintessential middle-class Englishman of his generation, but this did not indicate parochialism. His special subject at university had been Renaissance Italy. As an emerging politician his domestic preoccupations were first expanded through the Simon Commission, giving his politics an imperial focus. Only in the post-1931 Labour Party was he forced to concentrate on European affairs. He was concerned with weakening of democratic politics across much of Europe and inevitably with the threat to security posed increasingly by German ambitions.

As Prime Minister his priorities were initially with European reconstruction and subsequently with the division of Europe along the fracture of the Cold War. In Greece his government effectively continued the Coalition policy of supporting the Right against the Communists in what would become a civil war. He had little optimism about the left's prescription that Britain give a lead to a European third force as an alternative to American capitalism and Soviet communism. Once his early willingness to explore Soviet intentions had died he became committed specifically to the defence of Western Europe with the thorough involvement of the Americans. Milestones were the advent of Marshall Aid, the Berlin blockade and the emergence of the NATO. Tolerance was shown towards anti-Communist authoritarian regimes in Spain and Portugal. In contrast the Attlee government was hostile towards the Italian and French Communist Parties, the strongest forces on their national lefts.

Concern with European security was not complemented by any great interest in cross-national institutions within Western Europe. Attlee was at best cool towards the Schuman Plan for the Franco-German pooling of coal and steel, while other ministers were hostile. For these politicians, most born in the 1880s, the Commonwealth was a dominant concern. The government's marginality to the first moves towards European integration is understandable. So is Attlee's later opposition to British applications to join the Common Market.

a cross-party approach. Japan's entry into the war and the fall of Singapore had led British ministers to consider a new India initiative. Attlee and Cripps had become members of a new India Committee of the War Cabinet. Frequently this had been chaired by Attlee rather than Churchill. The Cripps Mission of March–April 1942 had offered early elections for a constituent assembly that would construct a new constitution, but Cripps had been unsuccessful. Mistrust of the British, differences between Congress and the Muslim League, divergent views within the Churchill Coalition, all had played their part. When Congress in response had launched the Quit India Campaign in August 1942 Attlee had chaired the War Cabinet in Churchill's absence. Backed by Cripps and Bevin he had endorsed a policy of detention of Congress leaders. In July 1945, in the eyes of recently released Congress politicians, not least Nehru, the reputations of senior Labour ministers were seriously tarnished.

The new government's Secretary of State for India, Pethick Lawrence, had recently moved to the Lords. A benign and somewhat vague idealist, he dreamed of an agreed solution. Both his peerage and personality meant that other ministers would provide the public face of policy. The government's first optimistic step was to resurrect the Cripps offer of 1942. Optimism owed much to ignorance. Ministers were understandably reluctant to acknowledge the damage done by their support for repression. They disregarded the strength of the Muslim League and therefore the elusiveness of an agreed outcome. They had to acknowledge the radicalising impact of the war on Indian opinion and the associ-

*I hope that the Indian people may elect to remain within the British Commonwealth ... If, on the other hand, she elects for independence, in our view she has a right to do so.*

ATTLEE

ated withering of British credibility. As with so much else, the limits of the economically feasible had to be addressed. Indian demands and British Labour expectations meant that the challenge could not be avoided, but any government initiative would be from a position of weakness.

On 19 February 1946 Attlee made an unexpected announcement. There would be a Cabinet mission to India. Pethick Lawrence's idealism would be complemented by Alexander's support for great power claims, but Cripps, on grounds of intellect and experience, inevitably dominated the trio. The initiative lay not in London with Attlee but with Cripps through three months of tortuous negotiations, not least with the iconic but complex Gandhi. Attlee, in the Commons before the mission's departure, emphasised the openness of the agenda. *I hope that the Indian people may elect to remain within the British Commonwealth … If, on the other hand, she elects for independence, in our view she has a right to do so.*[27]

The fact of the mission indicated that the old Cripps offer was effectively superseded. Discussion could envisage the possibility of partition. The outcome was a statement published on 16 May. This attempted to balance Congress insistence on a strong central state with devolution effective enough to win the agreement of the Muslim League. A three-tier federation was proposed. The all-India level would conduct foreign affairs, defence, finance and communications, while the provinces could concede selected powers to provincial groupings that would provide an intermediate level. Formal acceptance by Congress and the Muslim League rested on divergent interpretations and proved temporary. Communal violence in Calcutta left 5,000 dead. The League initially abstained from an interim government, but then entered with the result that central government became paralysed.

Faced with mounting chaos the Viceroy, Lord Wavell,

proposed a breakdown plan for a phased British withdrawal. Effectively a soldier's response, ministers rejected this as politically impossible, an undignified departure followed by disorder, a major blow to British prestige that would be regarded as the beginning of the end for the British Empire. Such a melancholy sequence would make the government vulnerable to Conservative attacks. The lack of British capacity to influence events was all too obvious.

Attlee's distinctive contribution is frequently claimed to have come at this critical moment. The most basic element was a definite date for withdrawal, in effect a politician's version of Wavell's breakdown plan. In December 1946 the Cabinet's India Committee plus Wavell decided on 31 March 1948 as an appropriate date. This was put back to June when the policy was made public two months later. The evidence of those present suggests that Cripps, not Attlee, was the most influential voice in the decisive discussions. This appraisal would fit with Attlee's practice of leaving the initiative to the self-confident and the well-informed.

Wavell, although present at these deliberations, would not be involved in their implementation. Key ministers felt that he lacked the political flair and the positive relationships with Indian politicians essential for the delicate task of negotiation, that would be precipitated by the announcement of a date for the transfer of power. Attlee is widely credited with what proved to be the inspired choice of Mountbatten. He certainly made that claim. *It was my own thought entirely to choose Mountbatten to negotiate India's independence. I knew his record in the war, and I decided that he was the man to get good personal relations with India, which he did. He and I agreed entirely. I told him I wanted a man to end the British Raj. He wanted a definite date to bring the Indians up to scratch of decision.* [28] Attlee proposed Mountbatten's appointment to the King three days before the India

Committee decided on a deadline for the transfer of power. It appears that Cripps had already discussed, not least with Nehru, the possibility of Mountbatten replacing Wavell. The manner of Wavell's removal seemed characteristic of Attlee. The Viceroy complained of the fatal telegram's curt tone. In fact, a draft dismissal had been written by Cripps.

The Attlee–Cripps relationship was the basis for the shift in government policy. Predictably the unexpected commitment to a calendar produced ministerial objections. Bevin's involvement had been marginal, but he was anxious about the wider implications. 'I am against fixing a date ... Not only is India is going but Malaysia, Ceylon and the Middle East, with a tremendous repercussion on the African territories ... We appear to be trying nothing but to scuttle out of it without dignity or plan.'[29] This opposition preceded by a few days Bevin's final argument with Attlee on Middle East policy. But over India Attlee's was the last word. *If you disagree with what is proposed, you must find a practical alternative. I fail to find one in your letter.*[30] In the endgame Attlee, supported by Cripps, appeared as the personification of the government's policy. Congress in the last resort preferred a strong Indian state and partition to formal unity without effective central institutions. Dominion status embraced two governments, India and Pakistan. The timetable telescoped. The transfer date became 15 August 1947.

Bevin's criticisms had included anxiety about the domestic implications of a chaotic withdrawal. This proved unfounded. Conservative concern about setting a date gave way to effective bipartisanship when the Independence Bill rapidly passed into law in July. To some extent such agreement indicated the absence of a credible alternative. It also represented the government's characterisation of a withdrawal in reality necessitated by economic weakness. Necessity was transformed into a narrative of emancipation through stages beginning with the Montagu–Chelmsford reforms of 1919. Attlee had played his part in these earlier developments. The actions of his government were presented as a final instalment in a lengthy process, not an improvised response to the unavoidable and seemingly intractable. This final instalment was expressed in the language of high-minded principle. The British had brought the prospect of democracy to India. The act of independence was a final establishment of 'our honesty of purpose'.[31] The words were Cripps'. Their credibility depended also on Attlee's combination of progressive politics, modesty and social conservatism. He could present the outcome as enlightened and yet resting on a tradition of service in India that was idealised but credible. But this passage from India meant a substantial human tragedy. In the violence that came with partition up to a million died. But the British later compared what they remembered with subsequent imperial disasters. Compared with the French in Algeria and Indo-China, Attlee and India allowed the British to feel good about their own enlightenment.

Attlee was a marginal figure in his government's other great imperial crisis. Following the collapse of the Ottoman Empire, Britain administered Palestine under a League of Nations mandate. A commitment to a Jewish national home had been made in the Balfour declaration of 1917. Jewish immigration between the wars in relatively small numbers was followed by communal violence between Jews and Arabs. Officially Labour Party sympathies were Zionist. Poale Zion, the Jewish Socialist Labour Party, was affiliated to the party as a socialist society, and Morrison, Dalton, Bevan and Shinwell all championed the cause. Typically Attlee was not an enthusiast. But in 1944, the party backed a level of Jewish immigration that would make them the majority.

# Attlee and America

Attlee's lifetime saw the rise of the United States to become a dominant world power. Born during the presidency of the largely forgotten Chester Arthur, Attlee's early life saw the economic rise of the post-Civil War US and the imperial ambition evident in the war with Spain. His formative years as a national politician were characterised by the American isolationism that followed the political defeat of Woodrow Wilson and in the depressed thirties by the Roosevelt New Deal. Many on the British left viewed the New Deal with scepticism as a doomed attempt to rescue capitalism. Attlee was perhaps more open-minded.

Attlee's experiences in the Churchill Coalition made him aware of the tough realism of American policy towards its British ally. As Prime Minister the rapid termination of Lend-Lease provided early corroborative evidence. The terms attached to the subsequent loan underscored the reality of British dependence. Attlee combined insistence on his government's socialist credentials with an emphasis on a shared Anglo-American inheritance of language, political ideas and ethics. He appealed to a progressive America. Yet Attlee's belief in the necessity of American support in the defence of Western Europe was without illusion. There were points of friction between the allies, not least over Palestine where Attlee felt that British responsibility was subverted by the complexities and unpredictability of American policymaking. Moreover the need for American involvement in Europe led to British backing for their ally in the Far East despite belief that US policy was often mistaken. Attlee's flight to Washington in December 1950 entered Labour mythology as an intervention that prevented a potentially disastrous expansion of the Korean conflict. Yet the principal legacy was British acceptance of an economically damaging rearmament programme.

Attlee's largely illusion-free backing of the US contrasts with the emotional attachments of Gaitskell and Blair. Yet the consequences of the Attlee Government's commitment have been profound. Alongside the health service the Anglo-American relationship is one of the government's most durable legacies.

Many anticipated that a Labour government would be pro-Zionist, but they were wrong. The subsequent tragedy became identified closely with Bevin and the Foreign Office. The latter's position had been traditionally pro-Arab. The co-operation of Arab states, however reactionary, was seen as essential to British influence in the Middle East. With the withdrawal of British forces from most of Egypt, Palestine acquired increased importance as a potential base, not least for the protection of oil supplies. Bevin's impact on this policy remains controversial. His crude and insensitive humour and his tactless comments fuelled accusations of anti-Semitism. The enormity of the Holocaust had given a terrible urgency to the desperation of Jews rotting in displaced persons' camps across Europe. Unappreciative of the force of Jewish nationalism, this seasoned negotiator reacted angrily to the inflexibilities of the contending parties. In Cabinet Attlee backed Bevin. The Colonial Secretary from October 1946, Creech Jones, was a moderate Zionist but was overshadowed by Bevin. The concerns of other colleagues had little impact.

The government's Palestine policy was a chronicle of communal violence, repression and an unavailing search for a negotiated one-state solution, all underscored by British financial weakness. In February 1947 Bevin announced that the issue would be referred to the United Nations; in August a UN Committee produced a majority in favour of partition. On 29 November the UN General Assembly endorsed this position. By then the Cabinet had decided to quit Palestine. For Attlee at the critical meeting on 20 September the India example was appropriate. 'In his view there was a close parallel between the position in Palestine and the recent situation in India. He did not think it reasonable to ask the British administration in Palestine to continue in present conditions, and he hoped that salutary results would be produced by a clear announcement.'[32]

Yet when the British left in May 1948 their decision had not had a catalytic effect. Out of the ruins came an immediate declaration of the State of Israel and fighting between Jews and Arabs. Attlee's marginality, despite his endorsement of Bevin's failed policy, protected his reputation.

The Palestinian imbroglio had a damaging effect on Anglo-American relations. Truman was sympathetic to Zionism, and some of his advisors were passionately committed. Jewish interests had influence in sections of the Democratic Party. Decision-making in Washington could be complex and confused. Presidential initiatives could mean outcomes at odds with British preferences. Eleven minutes after the British mandate ended on the night of 14/15 May 1948, Truman recognised the State of Israel. This precipitate act caused widespread dismay within the UN. In London Ernest Bevin expressed what was diplomatically labelled his extreme displeasure. On an earlier occasion Attlee had made his anger clear. In early October 1946 British negotiations with Arabs were at a delicate stage and there was some hope of involving Jews in the discussions. On the eve of Yom Kippur Truman appeared to endorse the objective of a viable Jewish state. For Attlee, Truman had raised Jewish expectations and thus possibly destroyed any opportunity for negotiations.

*I have received with great regret your letter refusing even a few hours grace to the Prime Minister of the country which has the actual responsibility for the government of Palestine in order that he might acquaint you with the actual situation and the probable results of your action. These may well include the frustration of the patient efforts to achieve a settlement and the loss of still more lives in Palestine.*[33]

This sad episode underscored a basic feature of the government's position. In the Middle East as elsewhere British viability depended on American support.

# Chapter 5: 'Annus Horribilis'

1947 was the Attlee government's 'annus horribilis'. Domestic affairs were no longer characterised by self-confidence, and instead successive crises brought lack of direction, ministerial squabbles and the one occasion when Attlee's position as Prime Minister seemed vulnerable. The first drama was a meteorological misfortune. Appalling weather began in late January and lasted well into March. A fuel crisis meant the rationing of electricity, industrial shutdown and temporary unemployment. But behind the bad luck the underlying coal shortage suggested an unwelcome verdict: ministerial claims about the effectiveness of planning were more rhetoric than substance. Shinwell, the responsible minister, had expressed groundless optimism about fuel stocks. The calamity precipitated forceful criticism by colleagues but Attlee, the supposedly effective 'butcher', seemed reluctant to move him.

No sooner had the snow melted than an increasingly unsure Cabinet divided over steel nationalisation. Argument lasted from April until August. Coal was already nationalised, and within the party the railways, much road transport, electricity and gas were uncontroversial candidates, but for some ministers steel was different. The dispute came to symbolise broader concerns about the extent and character of the government's professed commitment to socialism. Aneurin Bevan, Dalton and less forcefully Cripps favoured public ownership as presented in the 1945 manifesto, while the responsible minister John Wilmot, backed by Morrison, advocated a compromise. The industry's existing structure should be retained but the government would exercise its right to the compulsory purchase of shares. Initially Attlee and several others appeared to endorse this option. However, subsequent discussions in late July and early August resulted in a continuing commitment to public ownership but the postponement of legislation for a year. Those favouring postponement and the few advocates of immediate action probably made a bare Cabinet majority. Characteristically Attlee had shifted to support the majority position. The tactic ensured Cabinet cohesion but the underlying issue, the extent of public ownership and its significance for socialism, would bedevil the party for many years.

As ministers patched up a decision over steel, they were haunted by the spectre of 1931. From early in the year Dalton had urged his colleagues to address a deteriorating balance of payments. The situation signposted a premature exhaustion of the American loan, but his ministerial colleagues showed indifference or prioritised departmental interests. Cuts in military expenditure were parsimonious. Attlee contributed nothing to the increasingly desperate debate. The start of convertibility on 15 July brought an even sharper run on the dollar reserves and a fall in stock values. Ministers drew uncomfortable parallels with an August crisis 16 years earlier. The immediate threat was addressed on 20 August when the Americans agreed to the suspension of convertibility. The underlying economic problem remained.

The economic crisis precipitated a Cabinet crisis. Ministerial loss of confidence and lack of direction bred recriminations. Morrison had been seriously ill earlier in the year and his lack of feel for economic planning was all too obvious.

Dalton was no longer the optimistic Chancellor with a song in his heart, but had become beleaguered and frustrated. Attlee was criticised widely. In the summer of 1947, he appeared to many, not as a master tactician, but as inadequate, unimaginative and overwhelmed by events. His Commons speech on the convertibility crisis failed to inspire. A subsequent meeting of the parliamentary party heard much generalised dissatisfaction. Senior colleagues muttered about lack of leadership and listened to those retailing and inflating backbench gossip.

Fevered July days had brought rumours that Bevin would head a coalition government. Within the Labour Party, George Brown and Patrick Gordon Walker, Parliamentary Private Secretaries to Dalton and Morrison respectively, attempted to organise backbenchers against Attlee. When Brown mentioned this to Dalton, the latter suggested that the critics should make a row at a party meeting. Bevin subsequently complained to Dalton about the shortcomings of colleagues, not least the indecision of Attlee, and Dalton with typical indiscretion raised the possibility of Bevin replacing the Prime Minister. The movement rapidly died. If Bevin had had any thought of challenging Attlee, this soon vanished. Instead he shifted the responsibility for any conspiracy to the all-too-credible Dalton. He expostulated to Brown – 'You are acting as office boy for that bastard Dalton! I don't want to see you again.'[1]

If a revolt of parliamentary peasants had collapsed, perhaps a coup could succeed. This time the instigator was Cripps. Early in September he approached Dalton with a plan. They, together with Morrison, should see Attlee in order to persuade him to resign in favour of Bevin. Cripps' real purpose was to reform economic planning. Bevin would be more decisive than Attlee. Morrison must relinquish his planning responsibilities. He, Cripps, should take them over. Dalton should move to the Foreign Office and Attlee should shift to the Treasury. Cripps' agenda was typically flavoured with political naivety. Why should Morrison conspire to replace Attlee with a man who despised him? Was there any evidence that Bevin would be interested? Even if he were, why should such a tough operator endorse Cripps' allocation of responsibilities? Predictably Morrison agreed that Attlee should be replaced; equally predictably he thought that he should be the replacement. On 9 September Cripps saw Attlee, not as one of a trio, but alone. He presented his proposals, and Attlee calmly demolished them. He knew nothing about economics and could not be Chancellor. Bevin wanted to stay at the Foreign Office. Bevin and Morrison could not work closely together. But Attlee acknowledged that economic planning must be reformed and he offered Cripps a new assignment, as Minster of Production. Cripps accepted. Instead of precipitating a resignation, his own or Attlee's, he had been promoted.

Once again Attlee had demonstrated his political dexterity. He and Bevin were undamaged; Cripps was strengthened. Morrison had lost his economic responsibilities, but might well have been relieved. Dalton, already bruised by crisis, had acquired a powerful colleague. Within a few weeks a trivial indiscretion led to his replacement by Cripps. Attlee's skilful handling of this challenge would have been facilitated by persistent rumours about a possible coup. Cripps' ultimatum was no surprise. Such a situation brought out Attlee's strengths. He could keep his nerve, fortified by the knowledge that his senior colleagues could never agree on an alternative. The aftermath of the crisis brought a long-anticipated ministerial reshuffle. Several veterans retired from the junior ranks, allowing some scope for 1945 entrants. Shinwell was moved out of the Cabinet into the War Office and replaced at Fuel and Power by a talented and ambitious Wykehamist, Hugh Gaitskell. His promotion and Harold Wilson's entry into Cabinet foreshadowed future conflicts.

From November 1947 the economic credibility and electoral prospects of Attlee's government were dependant heavily on Cripps. He addressed the dollar shortage through the budget, shifting resources from domestic consumption into exports. Cripps has been characterised as the first Keynesian Chancellor, and more familiarly as the personification of austerity. At critical moments, Bevin's role was vital. In February 1948 the TUC General Council responded critically to a White Paper on Personal Incomes, Costs and Prices. Lack of consultation threatened hope of union co-operation. Bevin joined Attlee and other ministers at a meeting of the General Council's Economic Crisis Committee. The result was TUC acceptance of wage restraint. This commitment lasted despite difficulties for over two years. The compact highlighted the government's credibility in trade union circles. Sam Watson, leader of the Durham Miners, claimed 'If I were confronted with the defeat of the Government or the reduction of wages, I should advocate a reduction of wages to save the Labour Government'.[2] The Cold War also facilitated agreement since Communist-influenced unions opposed wage restraint. Attlee's own political style fitted well with the politics of austerity and the hard slog, but he remained marginal to the complexities of economic management as a response to Cripps' erudition showed. *I am not highly skilled in these matters and some of my colleagues are in like case. I think that we should welcome an explanation of this subject in Cabinet before the lines of the Budget are settled.*[3]

*I am not highly skilled in these matters and some of my colleagues are in like case. I think that we should welcome an explanation of this subject in Cabinet before the lines of the Budget are settled.*

ATTLEE

This age of austerity inevitably gave critics many opportunities to emphasise the burden of rationing and economic controls, especially when exacerbated by ministerial incompetence. Conservative appeals to housewives and to the alleged miseries of the middle class became more effective. Ministerial responses in the language of fair shares were less plausible when some Labour politicians appeared to fall below their proclaimed ethical standards. In October 1948, the press began to carry stories that some ministers had been receiving gifts in return for favourable treatment. Opponents proclaimed that such corruption was inescapable within a controlled economy. In terms of ethics, there was a simple issue of hypocrisy. Rumours centred on the Board of Trade, especially a junior minister John Belcher. Dalton, a second junior minister Charles Key, and a prominent trade unionist George Gibson were also the subjects of allegations. There opened up a vista of rhetorically self-righteous Labour politicians socialising with and doing favours for those whom ministers denounced as non-productive parasites, in the contemporary idiom 'spivs'.

Attlee responded quickly and decisively. Taking only the advice of the Lord Chancellor, Jowitt, he appointed a Tribunal of Inquiry under Mr Justice Lynskey. Against Cabinet advice, the Attorney General Sir Hartley Shawcross conducted the whole case. A political time-bomb was defused. A potentially damaging scandal became 'sub judice', and the complex evidence was widely regarded as tedious. Most crucially for the government, any corruption would be ascribed to individual failings, not labelled a consequence of government policy. Belcher and his wife were subjected to severe questioning by Shawcross. The Report censured him; he resigned his seat. His misdemeanours were venial, but his was the sacrifice that could protect the government's reputation for propriety. Gibson resigned from the Board of the Bank of England, although some ministers felt this was unnecessary. The official Conservative response drew a line under a sensation that had promised much but yielded little. The Lynskey affair established a benchmark for prime-ministerial intolerance of colleagues' failings. Almost 15 years later at the time of the Profumo scandal, some Labour politicians claimed a decline from what they called the Attlee standard. Attlee's shrewdness had protected the credibility of the government, but concern about austerity remained a powerful electoral challenge.

The deepening of the Cold War meant that bipartisanship on international affairs strengthened. Tensions became much more focused on Europe, the Communist takeover in Czechoslovakia, the containment of Communism in Italy and Germany and the Berlin airlift. American involvement in Europe intensified, both militarily and with the development of Marshall Aid. Attlee's rhetoric became strongly anti-Communist. He dismissed the Russian version: *Communism is an old word with very respectable antecedents. This particular form of Communism is Russian Communism, an economic doctrine wedded to the policy of a backward state, which has but very slight appeal to those who have experience of Western civilisation but makes a strong appeal to backward people who have never known anything better … It is rather like the attitude of the early adherents of Islam. Everyone else outside is an infidel.*[4]

By early 1948 for many there seemed no scope for neutrality or even complexity. For many erstwhile critics the Communist takeover in Czechoslovakia removed any ambiguity. Attlee was unequivocal. *The great fight was on and we are all enlisted in it.*[5] Any suggestion that Soviet intentions and fears be sympathetically explored was confined to the dustbin of history. Instead in March 1948 Attlee announced a policy of removing Communists and Fascists from sensitive positions within the Civil Service. Existing procedures already covered espionage. The concern was to strengthen an association between Communism and treason. The area of legitimate dissent was narrowing.

Such sentiments could affect Labour ministers' approach to industrial disputes. When London dockers struck in the summer of 1948, Attlee broadcast an appeal to end the strike, speaking as one who had lived in Docklands for many years. He spoke in the language of community and principle: *This strike is not a strike against capitalists or employers. It is a strike against your mates; a strike against the housewife; a strike against the ordinary common people who have difficulties enough to manage on their shilling's-worth of meat and the other rationed commodities.*[6] This appeal was legitimate and compelling within labour culture. A year later ministers from Attlee downwards hunted for Communist agitators and conspirators to explain unofficial strikes on the docks and railways. Such zeal could substitute for an adequate appreciation of how government measures had affected workers' experiences. The government had reformed the system of employment in the docks. However, the consequential National Dock Labour Scheme did not become acceptable simply because the Transport Workers' leadership insisted that it was. Railway nationalisation changed neither the pattern of management nor the struggles with obsolescent equipment that testified to decades of under-investment. Attlee and his colleagues' appeals to a higher social ethic could be persuasive, but they could ignore the discrepancy between Labour aspirations and the facts of working class experience. Allegations about Communists simply evaded the problem. Loyalty to Labour could be loyalty despite ... as much as loyalty because ...

Despite the effectiveness of Cripps' policies, the balance of payments and the state of the dollar reserves remained critical. In the summer of 1949 another financial crisis resulted in a September devaluation. At a crucial period Cripps' deteriorating health took him on leave for six weeks. Attlee formally replaced him, but the key political figures were three younger men, Gaitskell, Wilson and another Wykehamist, Douglas Jay. Gaitskell, in particular once persuaded of the need for devaluation, took a leading role in discussions with Attlee and other senior ministers. A conclave at Chequers captured the style and the decline of the party's senior figures.

'We ... talked for two and a half hours. It was a depressing occasion. The argument rambled along; sometimes about devaluation itself; sometimes about the date. The PM did not intervene at all but sat at his desk doodling and listening to the argument. Stafford was quite out of touch ... The Foreign Secretary swayed this way and that, and every now and then we were treated to a long monologue on some event of recent history such as how he had handled the flour millers in 1924, and what he had said to Ramsay MacDonald in 1931 etc. It was very hot and the room is a very small one.'[7]

Thus Gaitskell, a younger man in a hurry, portrayed senior figures. Yet once the devaluation had been implemented and the Cabinet discussed the extent and incidence of consequential expenditure cuts, Attlee's managerial strengths could be employed. He expressed pleasure with the outcome. *The whole thing is in great contrast to the 1931 business. I think that the Party and the electorate have learned a lot since then.*[8] In fact Cabinet discussions had been acrimonious. Alexander had predictably opposed cuts in the Defence budget, while Aneurin Bevan had threatened resignation if the Health estimates were attacked. Morrison reacted suspiciously to Bevan's claims. Although the Health Service represented the most rapidly expanding element in government spending, it escaped with minimal damage, unlike Bevan's other responsibility, housing. As soon as the Cabinet had reached agreement, Bevan wrote to Attlee protesting about the 'gorged and swollen defence estimates'. Attlee replied, *these adjectives are not based on knowledge.*[9]

In the last months of 1949 an election could not be far away. The moment provides a vantage-point for an assessment of the first Attlee government. Maintenance of full employment contrasted with the brittleness of the post-1918 boom. Economic constraints had not prevented the development of an extensive welfare system. Its most admired achievement, the National Health Service, was linked indissolubly with a minister who remained in significant respects an outsider. A succession of public ownership measures had culminated in legislation for the steel industry. Controversial within the Cabinet, it was opposed fiercely by the Conservatives and still faced the delaying power of the Lords. Ministerial self-congratulation was understandable but could involve an element of self-deception. Public ownership had not changed the position of workers in those industries to a significant degree. The redistributive impact of government policies was much less radical than supporters and critics claimed. Each had a vested interest in exaggeration. From 1947 the reforming vigour of the administration had declined, in part because of successive crises, in part because of ideological uncertainty. Should the fulfilment of the agenda of Attlee's generation be succeeded by further socialist measures, or did these achievements necessitate, in the contemporary term, consolidation? The verdict remained open, but Morrison, ever active in party policy-making, persuasively advocated consolidation. Attlee characteristically sought to hold the balance.

By 1949 the alliance with the United States, with all that it entailed in terms of policy, allies, adversaries and approved discourse, was central to government strategy. The North

Atlantic Treaty Organisation (NATO) was the coping-stone. Certainly the development of the alliance was despite significant disagreement most vehemently over Palestine, but disturbingly from 1949 over China and the Far East. These disagreements were subordinated to the basic precept that the imperatives of European security made the alliance essential. British illusions concerned the viability of Great Power expectations and the durability of the Empire. The transfer of power in India had acquired iconic status; it did not presage an imminent and broader decolonisation.

The impact of the American alliance was not restricted to foreign policy. Internalisation of Cold War beliefs and values combined with visceral loyalism and a chastened assessment of economic possibilities to produce a less radical party culture. The American labour attaché reflected positively on the party's 1949 conference. Leaders had 'grown in maturity'; delegates were 'prepared to follow their leaders wherever they felt it necessary to take them'. The 'Marxist strand of thought' barely figured. There were 'no naïve illusions about the world'. 'Traditional conceptions such as nationalisation and the redistribution of wealth were being replaced by a realistic conception of economics.'[10] Labour MPs' lack of enthusiasm for NATO suggested that such traditional conceptions remained influential, but the assessment captures a relative absence of controversy within the party. It also signposts how ministers were under continual pressure to reduce economic controls and to allow more autonomy for private industry.

The achievements of Attlee's first administration were significant and ambiguous. They were also more contested than some commentators have suggested. Conservative acceptance of welfare provision and full employment was electorally inescapable, but this was combined with appeals to 'set the people free', and attempts to exploit middle class resentment at what seemed an enhanced status for the working class.

When the general election was called for 23 February 1950, most ministers expected a smaller but comfortable majority. Attlee anticipated a close result. An extensive redistribution of constituencies would inevitably reduce Labour's strength. Inner cities were declining in population and their parliamentary representation was cut. Stepney's three seats became one. Attlee moved to another safe seat, West Walthamstow. The government's by-election record was encouraging: despite periods of unpopularity no seat won in 1945, however marginal, had been lost. Attlee's unostentatious national tour, chauffeured by his wife, attracted much favourable attention. Speaking in small towns, taking tea in Co-op cafes, the style and the appeals to public spirit personified Labour's sense of respectability and egalitarianism. The result was a wafer-thin majority of six that disguised a Labour lead in the popular vote of over 750,000 (2.6 per cent). On a significantly higher poll, Labour's vote increased by more than one and a quarter million; Conservative support grew by more than double that amount. Turnout was spectacularly high at 84 per cent; for many electors the outcome clearly mattered. Society was divided but not adversarial; so much for claims about the straightforward construction of a post-war consensus. Labour's working-class vote held firm especially in areas of traditional strength. The party's support declined in the southeast and more broadly amongst that middle class minority who had voted Labour in 1945. In Wales the number of Labour MPs actually increased, but across London, the South of England and East Anglia it fell by 54. Any expectation that Labour had become the dominant party was dead.

Attlee's second government showed significant changes, but not at the most senior level. Only one Cabinet minister, the Colonial Secretary Arthur Creech Jones, had been defeated, and Attlee seemed relieved.

*Despite much hard work and devotion he had not appeared to have a real grip of administration in the Colonial Office. He was bad in the House and contributed nothing to Cabinet, so I was not altogether sorry to have the chance of replacing him by Jim Griffiths who had proved himself a first rate administrator and added weight to the TU side in the Cabinet.*[11]

A second post-war entrant, Patrick Gordon Walker, joined the Cabinet at Commonwealth Relations while Shinwell returned to the Cabinet after two and a half years, this time to Defence. The most significant change proved to be outside the Cabinet. An ailing Cripps was given support by Gaitskell as Minister of Economic Affairs.

A majority of six was regarded as having no long-term viability. Controversial measures were ruled out. The election result was a fillip for advocates of consolidation, and a setback for those who urged more radicalism. Yet when the National Executive and senior ministers met in May to discuss the election results, the party secretary Morgan Philips and the Durham Miners' leader Sam Watson asserted that Morrison's consolidation strategy would divide the party. Bevan and the radicals were effectively backed by those who emphasised harmony in a difficult situation. Attlee was a typically quiet member of this group. The Parliamentary Party seemed in good heart, prepared to dig in and bridge divisions in the interests of survival. But on 25 June 1950, everything changed.

Early on that morning forces from Communist North Korea crossed the 38th Parallel into South Korea. The consequential three years of war reduced Korea to a ruin, involved the major powers and aroused fears of a wider conflagration. Much about the war's origins remains controversial. Chinese Communist and Soviet leaderships knew of an impending invasion, but a focus on the immediate trigger neglects much. Korea had been annexed as a Japanese colony in 1910. Leading nationalists had been exiled. Japan's defeat in 1945 had brought *de facto* partition along the 38th Parallel, a demarcation between American and Soviet spheres. Thus Korea became marked by Cold War antagonisms in a climate of post-liberation eagerness for political unity and economic and social reforms. In the south progressive movements were crushed. From 1948 the South Korean regime was headed by Syngman Rhee, a repressive anti-Communist, an American creation who could embarrass his creators yet could not be disowned. Initially Korea might have seemed a remote backwater, but the victory of the Chinese Communists in 1949 made the Far East central to Cold War concerns. The Americans continued to back the defeated Chiang Kai-Shek regime in its Formosan redoubt. For Americans smarting from the 'loss' of China, 25 June 1950 could seem a significant moment in an extensive and co-ordinated campaign of aggression.

The Attlee government had serious differences with American Far East policy. It had given 'de facto' recognition to the new Chinese regime, reflecting concern about British economic interests, the security of Hong Kong and the conciliation of Asian, especially Indian, opinion. Yet the government immediately backed the United States at the United Nations in condemnation of North Korean aggression. Memories of the failure of collective security in the 1930s were fresh. When the crisis was debated in the Commons,

*I never knew that an excuse for assaulting someone peacefully pursuing his way was that his character was not very good.*

ATTLEE

Labour opposition was minimal. Attlee was firm. He rejected the relevance of the South Korean regime's repressive internal policies. *I never knew that an excuse for assaulting someone peace-fully pursuing his way was that his character was not very good.*[12]

A United Nations' resolution supporting assistance to South Korea led to American pressure for a British military contribution. Initially the Cabinet endorsed limited air and naval aid but accepted military advice against the commit-ment of land forces, but the pressure intensified as the North Koreans advanced. On 25 July the Cabinet agreed to a sig-nificant land contribution under UN auspices, but under the command of the American General Douglas MacArthur. As Attlee told the Cabinet, military concerns had been out-weighed by political considerations. Sir Oliver Franks, British ambassador in Washington, had been emphatic 'a negative decision would seriously impair the long-term relationship'.[13] Concern to stay in step with the Americans was not just expressed in the commitment of troops. By the end of August the Cabinet had agreed to a much expanded defence expendi-ture of £3,400 million down to 1954. One minister expressed principled concern about the abandonment of a strategy of containing Communism through social and political reforms rather than military methods. Aneurin Bevan's voice hinted at future arguments, but as yet he was alone in the Cabinet.

The drama of autumn 1950 escalated concerns about American policies and their consequences. Following the landing of US marines at Inchon in mid-September, the character of the war was transformed. In late September the Cabinet agreed to the UN, including British troops, advancing beyond the 38th Parallel into North Korea. Ignoring Chinese threats of intervention, MacArthur continued northwards proclaiming imminent victory and by late November UN troops approached the Yalu River, the border between North Korea and China. British concern grew about American, and specifically MacArthur's, intentions. On 26 November a mass Chinese offensive into Korea drove UN forces back in disarray and precipitated a critical episode in Anglo-American relations.

When the Cabinet discussed the chaos in Korea on 29 November concern was expressed about American policy and the mood of Labour backbenchers. Attlee attempted to prioritise commitments. *Their operations in Korea had been important as a symbol of their resistance to aggression; but Korea was not in itself of any strategic importance to the democracies, and it must not be allowed to draw more of their military resources away from Europe and the Middle East.*[14]

On the following day, as MPs debated foreign affairs, Truman, at a press conference seemed to suggest the possibility of the US using atomic weapons in Korea. These comments and their interpretation precipitated an intervention by Attlee that acquired mythical status. The Cabinet agreed rapidly that he should fly to Washington to meet Truman, their first meeting for five years. Two days later Attlee and Bevin met their French counterparts. His journey would express not merely British anxieties. On 3 December he flew to Washington and met Truman and the Secretary of State Dean Acheson, over a five-day period.

**Harry S Truman** (1884–1972) had been Vice-President for only 82 days when Franklin Roosevelt died in 1945 and he succeeded him as the 33rd President of the United States. The US dropped the two atomic bombs on Japan four months after he became President. His presidency saw the beginning of the Cold War, the McCarthy anti-Communist campaign and the 'loss' of China to Communism. He won the 1948 election against expectations, and during the Korean War sacked MacArthur for opposing his policies. He did not seek re-election in 1952 because of the unpopularity this caused him.

Acheson's recollection of Attlee's style was bleak. 'His thought impressed me as a long withdrawing melancholy sigh'. But the Secretary of State was more impressed by Attlee's skill as a negotiator. 'Mr Attlee's method of discussion was that of the suave rather than the bellicose cross examiner ... He soon led the President well onto the flypaper.'[15] When Attlee returned to Britain his visit was presented as a triumph. He had tempered American policy in Korea and towards China. There was no prospect of any use of the atomic bomb.

In fact the achievements were much more ambiguous. Arguably American policymakers became more aware of European concerns about their Far Eastern strategy. They were thoroughly negative, however, about the prospect of early negotiations with China which they dismissed as a Soviet satellite. They remained firm on the defence of Formosa and against the admission of representatives of Communist China into the UN. As American military expenditure grew so the price of strategically-vital raw materials increased. Attlee secured no effective response on the British request for a credible international policy on this problem. The sensational trigger for the visit, Truman's comments about the atomic bomb, was essentially covered in private conversations between President and Prime Minister. Truman's commitment to consult was not written in the final communiqué, which replaced 'consult' with 'inform'. Ernest Bevin remained sceptical about any significant change. Overall Attlee's private assessment was more realistic than the public congratulations.

One consequence was heightened American expectations about British military and diplomatic support. The Washington discussions had emphasised the continuing American commitment to the defence of Western Europe. One divisive consequence was US pressure for a West German contribution to this defence. The Cabinet agreed this in principle three days after Attlee's return from the United States. Its implementation would divide the party for the next four years. A more immediate and threatening consequence concerned renewed American demands for another expansion of defence expenditure. Attlee raised the issue in Cabinet on 18 December, but ministers reacted dismissively. The specific demand was economically impossible. The pressure continued. On 25 January 1951, the Cabinet reluctantly accepted a programme of £4,700 million for the three years to 1954. Aneurin Bevan opposed the new commitment on economic grounds. Gaitskell, Chancellor of the Exchequer since Cripps' retirement the previous October, highlighted the economic problems, not least for living standards and civilian investment. But the Chancellor was thoroughly committed to support of the Americans. He was backed by Morrison and Attlee.

This decision would have a traumatic effect upon the government. A concurrent and much more divisive Cabinet debate demonstrated that beyond the complexities of what was economically possible, emotions about American policy in the Far East ran high. On 20 January the US tabled a draft resolution at the United Nations declaring China guilty of aggression in Korea, and Chinese failure to withdraw could trigger economic and military sanctions. Ernest Bevin was unhappy about these consequences but felt that in the last resort support for the US was unavoidable. On 22 January, however, he went into hospital. His deputy Kenneth Younger opposed not only the resolution but the style of US policy.

When the Cabinet discussed the resolution, Younger favoured a vote against the American proposal. He was supported by eight ministers including Bevan, Dalton, Wilson and Addison. Attlee and Morrison favoured abstention. Only three spoke in favour of the USA, including the

Lord Chancellor Jowitt and the Secretary of State for Scotland Hector McNeil. But the most significant was Gaitskell. He was appalled at the decision. He later spoke to Addison, and to civil servants who were in his words 'completely horrified'. He met Attlee with Younger also present, when at Gaitskell's insistence a civil servant claimed that Younger had misrepresented Ernest Bevin's view in Cabinet. Gaitskell then saw Attlee alone. He had previously told one of his officials that he saw this as a resigning matter. Whether he mentioned this to Attlee is not recorded. 'I went over the same ground as I had with Addison. He listened in silence and we had a short discussion. He pointed out the difficulty arising from the fact that so many senior ministers ... held different views.'[16]

The prospect of an amended resolution allowed Attlee to advocate support for this at a subsequent Cabinet. Only Aneurin Bevan, Griffiths, Dalton and to some extent Chuter Ede continued to oppose the Americans.[17] This rapid-about turn followed pressure from Foreign Office officials. Their assessment was self-consciously realistic. American policy in the Far East was 'wrong headed, will unnecessarily add to the hostile forces ranged against us, and may precipitate a world war'. But 'we should accept the disagreeable conclusion, in the end, that we must allow the US to take the lead and follow, or at least not break with them.'[18] Within the Cabinet Gaitskell had been the decisive figure. With the resignation of Cripps and the incapacity of Bevin, here was a new force who networked effectively with influential ministerial colleagues and with officials, and was committed to support of the United States.

Gaitskell's formal eminence had begun in October 1950. On Cripps' resignation, he had risen from being Minister of Economic Affairs outside the Cabinet to the Chancellorship and to number four in the government. He had been the choice of Cripps and the subject of persistent lobbying by Dalton. Attlee saw his appointment as unproblematic, yet the promotion inevitably ruffled some ministerial feathers. Wilson, an economist with three years in the Cabinet, had legitimate expectations. Such a successful meritocrat could feel that Gaitskell epitomised the easy superiority of the educationally privileged. Aneurin Bevan probably had little personal interest in the post but complained forcefully about the appointment to Attlee and to others. Gaitskell's own competitiveness and limited range of sensibilities is evident from his diary. Bevan felt 'humiliated'; Wilson was 'inordinately jealous'.[19] Attlee had decided in all probability to block Bevan from any senior position. The critical moment might well have been the inauguration of the National Health Service in July 1948. Despite the resistance of the British Medical Association, urged on by many Tories, Attlee claimed the reform as a national and consensual achievement. In contrast Bevan compared the NHS with the Tories' inter-war record. So far as he was concerned they were lower than 'vermin'. The comment produced a cacophony of Tory abuse and a succinct rebuke from Attlee. Critical colleagues blamed Bevan's single sentence for the narrowness of the 1950 electoral success. This hyperbolic judgement reflected the clash between iconoclastic radicalism and a widespread ministerial desire not to give offence. Attlee's sympathies lay with the self-consciously respectable.

Even before October 1950 Bevan had experienced Gaitskell's zealous concern with tight control of Health Service finances. The NHS had to compensate for years of deprivation and had regularly exceeded its budget. Cripps had raised the issue of prescription charges. Bevan had formally accepted the principle but implementation had been deferred. From April 1950 a Cabinet committee attempted to control NHS expenditure. Tension between Gaitskell and Bevan heightened. On the committee and in the Cabinet Bevan was increasingly isolated.

In January 1951 Bevan's secondary status in the government was confirmed when Attlee transferred him from Health to Labour. Bevan later claimed to have obtained an assurance from the Prime Minister that Health Service charges would not be introduced. Experience of his new department made clear to Bevan the practical obstacles to the implementation of the expanded rearmament programme that he had already opposed in Cabinet. Before this crisis came to a head, Bevan had a further demonstration of his marginality. On 9 March, Attlee, after much procrastination, transferred Ernest Bevin from the Foreign Office. In little more than a month he was dead. Attlee's initial preference as a successor was for James Griffiths, but Gaitskell strongly advocated Morrison. Attlee was persuaded, in the event a mistaken choice. Bevan was never considered as a credible candidate.

Early in March Gaitskell raised the issue of Health Service charges with his three most senior colleagues, Attlee, Morrison and Ernest Bevin. On 15 March he presented his package to a small group chaired by Attlee. The Health Service Estimate would be held at £393 million, necessitating revenue from charges and a cut in hospital expenditure. Charges would be introduced on dentures, spectacles and prescriptions. Aneurin Bevan was forcefully opposed and was backed surprisingly by Ernest Bevin and also by Griffiths. Attlee was typically disinclined to intervene. The meeting ended without any decision. Gaitskell next sought support from senior colleagues. Ernest Bevin proposed a compromise – an expenditure ceiling raised to £400 million, no prescription charges but increased charges for the other two categories. The following day, 21 March, Attlee entered St Mary's Hospital for treatment for a duodenal ulcer. All subsequent Cabinets throughout the crisis were chaired by Morrison.

When Ernest Bevin's compromise was brought to the Cabinet, Aneurin Bevan opposed both on principle and in the context of an excessive defence programme. Opposition also came from Wilson and less clearly from Griffiths and Chuter Ede. Thereafter no resolution of the dispute was attempted. Even when Bevan, responding to heckling dockers at a Bermondsey meeting, insisted that he would not be a member of a government that imposed Health Service charges, nothing stirred.

Budget Day was 10 April. The previous morning the Cabinet discussed Gaitskell's budget proposals. Bevan insisted that the charges would mean his resignation. Gaitskell forcefully resisted any change. Fifteen ministers were present, and possibly four of them gave some support to Bevan and Wilson. The deadlock led Morrison to St Mary's where he asked for Attlee's opinion. Attlee's consequential letter to a reconvened Cabinet was typically vague. He emphasised the need for unity and the undesirability of an early election. Nevertheless he also indicated that Gaitskell should be supported. However, resistance continued.

Faced with continuing opposition Gaitskell raised the possibility of his own resignation. His aversion to compromise was evident in his reaction to a proposal made by George Tomlinson for the ceiling of £400 million to exclude any specific reference to the charges. Gaitskell characterised this as 'dangerous ... from my own point of view'.[20] This compromise could mean that the charges would never happen. It was also dangerous because Morrison found this proposal attractive and intended to mention it to Attlee.

Attlee met Bevan and Wilson on the morning of Budget Day. They found him sympathetic. But they were followed to his bedside by Gaitskell. Attlee suggested that he accept the Tomlinson proposal and indicated that his previous visitors have been willing to do so. Gaitskell was resistant.

'I had made up my mind that I would announce the charges and I refused to give way. I offered my resignation several times, and I thought as I listened to his arguments that he was going to accept it...Finally he murmured what I took to be '*Very well, you will have to go*'. In a split second I realised he had said '*I am afraid they will have to go*'.[21]

Gaitskell's hardness had won the point. With only a few hours till the Budget statement Attlee could not have permitted his resignation. In all probability Attlee hoped that once the charges had been announced, Bevan and Wilson would concede. Initial responses by Bevan seemed to give credence to this hope, but his and Wilson's attempts to secure postponement of the implementation of the charges met strong resistance from Morrison and Gaitskell. Their resignations were followed by that of a junior minister, John Freeman.

The affair was the most serious split within a Labour Cabinet other than the disintegration of August 1931. Bevan's resignation statement to the Commons widened the basis for disagreement beyond Health Service charges and defence expenditure to the future for British democratic socialism. The resignations strengthened the Labour left and began years of disputes and recriminations. Labour politicians would recall where each had stood in 1951 and throughout the frequently personalised feuds that followed.

The poisonous legacy inevitably poses the question whether the resignations were avoidable. The budget dispute was over a small amount of money. The defence programme that precipitated the crisis proved incapable of realisation. The specific issues signposted broader disputes. Health charges could be characterised as a breach of socialist principle or as an acknowledgement that all public provision must make a contribution in a context of economic stringency. It had been a strength of Attlee's leadership that he had been capable, often after a period of passivity, of focusing on precise and negotiable issues. In retirement Attlee claimed that his hospitalisation had been decisive. Morrison had failed to achieve a compromise. Yet Attlee's earlier behaviour had arguably contributed to this breakdown. Whatever the merits of individual appointments, he had seemed indifferent to Bevan's feelings as that proud architect of the government's finest achievement was viewed increasingly by some Cabinet colleagues as a problem. Equally the rise of Gaitskell was the ascent of someone who could seem hard and inflexible and who articulated the assured certainties of his social background. The clash between the product of Winchester and Oxford and the romantic one-time coalminer from Tredegar was one that Attlee was ill-equipped to understand. The underlying conflict went beyond specific issues and personalities. It concerned style, ideology and generational replacement. Personalised and thereby distorted, it offered a discordant requiem to the achievements of Attlee's generation.

In the aftermath of the ministerial resignations and in the context of an anticipated election, Attlee once more demonstrated his realism when faced with a crisis. Late in April 1951 a radical nationalist, Mohammed Musaddiq became Prime Minister of Iran. Five days later his government nationalised the Anglo-Iranian Oil Company commonly known as the Anglo-Persian. This followed abortive negotiations on the division of profits between the company and the previous Iranian government. The Anglo-Persian had its British community of 4,500 in the oilfields and around the Abadan Refinery.

Within the Cabinet some favoured military intervention. Morrison was one. He was new to the Foreign Office, uninformed about the issues and sensitive to public and parliamentary opinion. Shinwell at Defence was another. He visualised a row of dominoes. 'If Persia was allowed to get away with it, Egypt and other Middle Eastern countries would be encouraged to think they could try things on'.[22] In contrast, Attlee was realistic about what had happened and pessimistic about the possibility of an agreement.

*We must in view of the present highly charged atmosphere in Persia, and in particular of the emotional state of the Persian Prime Minister (who appeared to be on the lunatic fringe), agreed to accept the principle of nationalisation. It was no use making this a sticking point.*[23]

The Cabinet's decision against thoroughgoing military intervention came on 12 July. Military constraints, economic weakness and political considerations all pointed in this direction. The political concerns included uncertainty about domestic support, the danger of a hostile resolution at the United Nations and lack of American sympathy. Attlee emphasised the need to acknowledge the nationalism increasingly prevalent in the Middle East, and if possible, to come to terms with it. Musaddiq's success showed dissatisfaction with the corruption of previous rulers. If his government were removed, there was no reason to believe that a successor would be any better.

*If negotiations could be resumed, it would be wise to stress, not only our acceptance of the principle of Nationalisation, but also our willingness to operate the oil industry on behalf of the Persian Government, on a basis of friendly partnership; then we must not alienate genuine nationalist feeling in Persia.*[24]

However, the government, in the light of more optimistic military advice, came to believe that a phased withdrawal of personnel could be combined with the military retention of Abadan Island, a firm affirmation of British resolve. This strategy was neither adopted nor rejected by the Cabinet. Rather it was deferred, whilst an idiosyncratic minister, Richard Stokes, conducted abortive negotiations with Musaddiq. On 25 September the Iranian government gave British staff one week to leave the country. Two days later the Cabinet debated the use of the military at Abadan. Morrison opposed scuttle and surrender.

Attlee for once took the lead, arguing firmly against intervention. The objections were many, not least that military occupation of Abadan could strengthen Musaddiq's position. The clinching argument was a familiar one. 'In the light of the United States' attitude, force could not be used to hold the refinery … We could not afford to break with the United States on an issue of this kind.'[25]

*The result of this election is anybody's guess, depending largely on which way the Liberal cat jumps.*

ATTLEE

Once again here was the essential relationship without illusions. The British evacuation took place on 4 October. The next day Attlee made his first speech in the election campaign. He found immense crowds and great enthusiasm. Despite the resignations and recriminations the party fought an effective and united campaign. Its vote remained doggedly loyal. On a slightly lower but still exceptionally high poll, Labour recorded its best ever popular vote, marginally ahead of the Conservatives. But there had been a massive decline in Liberal candidates, only 109 compared with 475 in 1950. Attlee knew that *the result of this election is anybody's guess, depending largely on which way the Liberal cat jumps.*[26] The cat favoured the Tories. Labour lost 21 seats to them and one to a Liberal beneficiary of local Tory backing, whilst making two gains from the Liberals in rural Wales. The party had gained the most votes but had narrowly lost the election. It had performed better than had seemed likely in the aftermath of the resignations. Yet the subsequent improvement in the economy suggests a tantalising counterfactual: if only Labour had hung on in office into 1952?

When Labour MPs met after the Conservative victory Attlee was re-elected leader by acclamation. The subsequent years are typically regarded as a regrettable postscript to his leadership. Factional feuds consumed much energy. The consequential debris marked a generation. Attlee's search for consensus was disparaged by dedicated factionalists as an absence of leadership. The political generation that had controlled the party since 1931 was in evident decline. Ernest Bevin was dead, Cripps had resigned from Parliament and would soon die. Dalton was a relatively marginal figure. Morrison was regarded widely as the heir apparent, but his period at the Foreign Office had tarnished his reputation. Attlee would be over 70 by the next election. A move from Stanmore to a cottage in the Chilterns suggested thoughts of retirement. Yet he had been replaced as Premier by Churchill who was more than eight years his senior. Attlee's departure was inevitably discussed but was not viewed as imminent.

The Cabinet resignations had left serious tensions. The election campaign had been characterised by a prudential solidarity, but differences had been widened from the specifics of Health Service charges and the viability of an ambitious rearmament programme to claims about socialist virtue and its alleged abandonment. Some rhetoric was harsh and personalised. Beyond disputes about policy lay visceral appeals, the tribalism of social networks based on class, style, education and prejudices. Once in opposition there were no longer inhibitions concerning the survival of a Labour government with a small majority.

The most fraught controversies came on international affairs. These reflected the Cold War polarisation of the early 1950s – Korea, German rearmament, the hydrogen bomb. Controversies were fuelled by suspicion about American policy. On German rearmament high-minded sentiments were flavoured with crude nationalism. Often the precise issues were obscured by the acrimony. Attlee perhaps recalling the tortuous international debates of the1930s sought with some success to construct unifying formulae.

Domestic challenges were largely the consequence of achievement. Attlee's governments had carried out Labour's programme. Yet the post-war reforms appeared to have achieved many of the aspirations of the labour movement within a more regulated and humane capitalism. Was this enough or should future Labour governments press on? Most within Attlee's generation were committed in some sense to a gradual transformation of capitalism not least through an expanding public sector. Disagreements were about priorities and pace. In contrast some younger figures, notably Gaitskell and his close associates Douglas Jay and Tony Crosland, were developing a revisionism that focused on a realisation of values rather than the necessity for specific measures. Given the apparent effectiveness of Keynesian economics, this opened up the prospect that socialist values could be strengthened significantly within a mixed economy. During Attlee's last years as leader, this ideological problem was barely addressed.

Although ideological divisions were blurred, debates were often bitter. Many wished for reconciling strategies that could maintain unity. This was Attlee's priority. He was backed by James Griffiths, by the short-term Bevanite Harold Wilson and by a 'Keep Calm' group of MPs who emerged at critical moments to insist on the virtue of ambiguity. Attlee and others who sought reconciliation attracted criticism from zealots. On the left Bevan was charismatic, unpredictable and volcanic, a compelling orator who could blend polemic and philosophical speculation. He could personalise disputes and score spectacular own goals. His parliamentary supporters were linked by personal affinities and the kaleidoscope of sentiments that was the Labour left. On the right the dominant figure was initially Herbert Morrison. Gradually he was superseded by Hugh Gaitskell, almost 20 years his junior.

In background Gaitskell was not dissimilar to Attlee, but instead of Stepney Gaitskell had held an economics lectureship at University College London, and for war service Whitehall had taken the place of Gallipoli. Gaitskell for some personified the 1951 split. Prepared to ally with the tough disciplinarians within the trade unions, he revealed a hardness that Morrison in the last resort, lacked.

*The Bevanite squabble is a nuisance ... I am not unduly worried as I have seen four and twenty leaders of revolt.*

ATTLEE

Attlee's concern to hold the party together was combined with exasperation at Bevan's behaviour. *Too much ego in his cosmos*[27] was an early response to his resignation. Attlee often felt that the discord had shallow roots and was therefore manageable. The party conference at Morecambe in October 1952 combined grim weather, vigorous and sometimes confrontational debates and a Bevanite triumph in the elections to the Party's National Executive that meant the defeat of Dalton and Morrison. Attlee expressed *sang froid. The Bevanite squabble is a nuisance – very largely a matter of vanity, envy and dislike of responsibility. I am not unduly worried as I have seen four and twenty leaders of revolt.*[28]

Sometimes his responses employed examples from his earlier career. When Labour MPs voted in autumn 1952 to ban unofficial groups, in effect the Bevanites, Attlee drew a parallel with the disastrous trajectory of the Independent Labour Party, a party within a party. Perhaps Morecambe brought back memories of pre-war East End politics. *There has been a considerable infiltration of near Communists into the Constituency delegations ... There was quite an organised clique.*[29] Attlee's allegation was made in private. The previous day Gaitskell had made the same claim in a speech and was attacked as a witch hunter.

Attlee's commitment to reconciliation was demonstrated most thoroughly in the spring of 1955. Gaitskell, Morrison and their parliamentary and trade union allies attempted to expel Bevan from the party. Their immediate justification was an allegedly insulting intervention by Bevan in a Commons debate on nuclear weapons. The 'insult' was directed at Attlee who seemed reluctant to press for the draconian penalty endorsed by a majority of his senior colleagues. Attlee's evident lack of enthusiasm arguably influenced critical votes. Labour MPs resolved to withdraw the whip from Bevan but the majority was unimpressive. The National Executive fortuitously rejected expulsion by a majority of one. Attlee's lukewarm presentation of the case for withdrawing the whip and his opposition to expulsion exasperated hardliners. Attlee criticised Gaitskell. *You made me the spearhead of a policy in which I did not believe.*[30] Gaitskell felt that Attlee had let his colleagues down. One significant factor that had prevented expulsion was the expectation that a general election was imminent.

Labour had entered opposition with its electoral optimism more or less intact. The small Conservative majority in Parliament and Labour's lead in the popular vote suggested that loss of office was temporary. However, the Churchill government, largely out of electoral prudence, did little to overturn the Attlee government's reforms. Contrary to Labour's predictions the inequalities of the 1930s did not reappear. Labour failed to make any by-election gains. Indeed in mid-1953, the government gained a seat from the opposition, a feat last achieved in 1924.

The long-delayed replacement of Churchill by Eden was followed almost immediately by an election in May 1955. For the last time Attlee campaigned as leader. The contest lacked fire. Labour ended up with 18 fewer seats, and more significantly, over one and a half million fewer votes. The outcome presaged the end of Labour's second generation. Attlee's assessment acknowledged this. *In my constituency there was nobody under seventy in the committee rooms and they were doing the same old routine they had done for the last thirty years. Won't do at all.*[31]

*'Few thought he was even a starter*
*There were many who thought themselves*
*  smarter*
*But he ended PM*
*CH and OM*
*An earl and a Knight of the Garter.'*
ATTLEE

On 7 December 1955 and without ceremony he resigned as Party Leader. The election of his successor was decisive – Gaitskell won 157 votes, Bevan 70, Morrison 40. Arguably Attlee's retention of the leadership had guaranteed this final and humiliating defeat for his long-time rival. He rapidly went to the Lords as Earl Attlee. Shortly afterwards he became a Knight of the Garter. He had never had any objection to honours.

# Part Three

THE LEGACY

# Chapter 6: Assessment

Attlee's autobiography *As It Happened* was published in the spring of 1954. He sent a copy to his brother Tom with a typically deprecatory assessment. *I am afraid that it is not very good.*[1] Three years later the second volume of Hugh Dalton's less discreet memoirs provoked a characteristic comparison. *While I wrote The Acts, Dalton gave them Revelations.*[2] He subsequently dismissed Morrison's ghost-written autobiography as *A fine work of fiction.*[3] Thus ageing survivors of the 1945 Cabinet sought in diverse ways to mould their collective achievements, most thoroughly Shinwell whose longevity allowed him several attempts. One anonymous and vitriolic reviewer characterised Attlee's effort as 'loosely written, clumsily constructed, much of it as boring as the minutes of a municipal gas undertaking ... seldom has the absence of emotion been recollected in greater aridity.' One dismissive reference has, however, been decisively falsified: 'It seems improbable that anything of the man himself will survive the first hand memories of those who have worked with him.'[4] Instead, Attlee's stature has grown as later events have spawned new perspectives from which to reassess his career. As Labour returned to office under Harold Wilson, the minority MacDonald governments could be seen as a flawed overture to the Attlee government's achievements. For the politically sympathetic, the Attlee years could be viewed as a first instalment. But in the light of the Wilson and Callaghan years, the Attlee government could seem an inspirational exception – the one Labour government that did not disappoint its supporters. With the advent of Margaret Thatcher and the often-effective attack on the political order that had been established in the 1940s, progressives prized this vanishing world. However ambiguous the record, the Attlee achievements seemed a peak, not a base camp.

The combination of efficient chairmanship, a concern to reconcile differences and an ability to act decisively in some crises contrasted with successors who offered personalised and hectoring leadership, browbeat colleagues, identified with factions or were insensitive to party sentiments. Attlee was honest and realistic. In the political shambles and human tragedy that is Iraq such virtues, often expressed modestly and with brevity, become even more appealing. Ernest Bevin valued him as the only senior figure who could unite all his egotistical colleagues. He chose an apposite comparison: Attlee was 'our Campbell-Bannerman'.[5] The similarities were extensive. In 1898 Campbell-Bannerman had become leader of a divided and electorally pessimistic Liberal Party. After facing many difficulties he had led them to a massive electoral triumph. He was a reconciler, most notably when the Liberals split acrimoniously over the Anglo-Boer War. He could be tough: angered by British reliance in the later stages of the war on farm burnings and concentration camps he denounced them as methods of barbarism. Rich and socially conservative and with metronomic habits, he was in Liberal terms a radical. Faced with the need to construct a Cabinet in December 1905, he outfoxed supposedly smarter colleagues who had wished his removal to the Lords, yet once in office he delegated much to these ambitious and talented ministers. He even appointed a Welsh critic. Like Aneurin Bevan, Lloyd

George proved a risk worth taking. Attlee's premiership had a Liberal precursor to whom some Labour recruits from Liberalism looked back with nostalgia.

Such a comparison is illuminating, but equally Attlee must be located firmly in his own time. A comment by the American political scientist, Sam Beer, provides a valuable starting point. 'During the generation 1918–48, the Labour Party was an ideological and programmatic party based primarily upon the organised working class. Within these main conditioning forms of purpose and power, the party developed. They did not wholly or mechanically determine that development. The party had an organisational life with its own autonomy. Individuals and groups put forward new ideas and contested positions of influence. But these events occurred within the broad framework of Socialist purpose and trade union power.'[6] The political significance of Attlee and his peers rested on the rise of Labour to major party status by the early 1920s and to election as a majority government in 1945. From the vantage-point of this victory the process could seem an almost natural

**What Attlee said:**

**On Winston Churchill:** 'Trouble with Winston. Nails his trousers to the mast. Can't get down.'

**On Aneurin Bevan and Jennie Lee:** 'He needed a sedative. He got an irritant.'

**On Hugh Dalton:** 'Perfect ass. Always had to have a secret to tell someone.'

**On Harold Laski:** 'Rather saw himself too big, did Harold. Funny for a student of political science. He couldn't quite work the thing out.'

**On Ramsay MacDonald:** 'It is difficult to get at MacDonald's mind at any time. It is I think mainly fog now.'

**On Herbert Morrison:** 'Poor little man. Didn't know he was eaten away with ambition.'

**On Lord Halifax:** 'Queer bird, Halifax. Very humorous, all hunting and holy communion.

progression from the formation of the Labour Representation Committee in 1900 and the 30 Labour MPs of 1906 to the minority governments of the 1920s and the fulfilment of 1945. The electoral strength of the industrial working class could make the forward march of Labour seem almost inevitable. On this reading 1931 was a temporary setback.

This comforting history was a myth. In 1914 Labour's parliamentary strength was limited. It was dependant on local Liberal benevolence and challenged ideologically by Liberal proposals for economic and social modernisation. With Attlee on military service the Liberal Party was divided by wartime controversies and personalised quarrels at precisely the moment when the franchise was massively expanded and, trade union membership and self-confidence had rocketed. Attlee and his generation exploited and benefited from this opportunity, first on local councils, and then at Westminster. Similarly in the late 1930s Labour's electoral recovery from the 1931 disaster remained limited. A subsequent general election would have meant another decisive failure, and then in all probability Attlee would have been replaced, but the invasion of Poland postponed any election. The crisis of spring 1940 gave Labour an opportunity to reconstruct the range of the politically feasible and desirable. The rise of Labour and hence of Attlee was a complex and messy process characterised by suppressed alternatives. Each war remade the party system in a way that could not have been predicted on the last day of peace and in each case Labour was a beneficiary. War proved not so much the locomotive of history but as in Max Weber's metaphor 'the switchman'.

Attlee's socialism was effectively formed during his early years within the Stepney ILP. It owed much to 19th-century critics of industrialism and nothing to Marxism. His ethical socialism was complemented by his appraisal of the

# Attlee's significance

Attlee's reputation stands high amongst 20th-century prime ministers not least because of his personal qualities. He was honest and insisted on decent standards in public life. An ethical socialist who epitomised the conformism and respectability of Home Counties suburbia, he was the least ostentatious of prime ministers. His style complemented the egalitarian ethos of the People's War and the immediate post-war years. These qualities informed his approach to leadership. Attlee was a reconciler who sought and often achieved sustainable compromises between talented and egotistical colleagues. His style could engender criticism, yet mutterings about passivity and absence of leadership were answered by Attlee's ability to wrong-foot critics or to take decisive action at critical moments.

His prime ministerial inheritance was bleak. Popular expectations were high but the British economy had been devastated by six years of war. Yet the government's domestic record was impressive. Full employment, welfare reforms and the development of a public sector ensured the loyalty of many working class voters. Attlee and his colleagues identified themselves as socialists. Yet their achievement was a reformed capitalism.

Socialist rhetoric featured little in the government's international policy. Military victory had left faith in Britain's world role intact. The deepening Cold War meant a close relationship with the United States. The cost of rearmament threatened the government's domestic achievements and helped to produce damaging political divisions. Indian independence stood out as an issue where the fact of a Labour government made a difference.

Attlee's government has often been presented as the architect of a post-war consensus, but this is not how it seemed at the time. Middle class resentment was as evident as consensus. Although Attlee could be a reassuring figure his faith in fair play, epitomised in his affection for cricket, limited his appreciation of opponents' antagonism. The Attlee years appeal not just as achievement but also as myth, a comfortable account of gentlemanly reform carried out by decent people and accepted by all just like the decisions of an umpire.

British state during the 1914–18 War. National emergency had meant frequent departures from unregulated capitalism. Here was an achievement to build on. Similarly Attlee saw the imperatives of the inter-war Depression leading to erosions of capitalist competition even under the National Government. A second wartime emergency brought further advances in what Attlee would have characterised as socialist common sense. He and his Labour colleagues felt they were working with the historical grain. He was optimistic about the extent to which socialist solutions could become matters of consensus.

Such optimism was perhaps strengthened by his social conservatism. His respect for and comfort in rule-governed institutions – Haileybury, 'Univ', the South Lancashires – extended to the Labour Party. Each had its ceremonial. Attlee might have been politically identified as the 'Man from Limehouse', but he was also the 'Man from Metroland'. Living in suburban security he followed the conventions of his class. His family were central to his life, and politics never travelled home to Stanmore. Other than the inescapable obligations of a party leader, there was no political partying; nor were there the self-consciously cerebral debates and conspiracies of Hampstead.

His liking for ceremonial was evident both as Opposition Leader and as Prime Minister. Attlee enthusiastically endorsed the monarchy and welcomed pageantry. Two of his most widely-acclaimed parliamentary speeches were made on the deaths of George V and George VI. The latter's death in February 1952 was one of the few occasions when Attlee's parliamentary colleagues saw him visibly upset. As Prime Minister his relationship with the King had been cordial and formal, between two quiet men who had shared a concern for the well-being of working-class boys. For a conservative monarch anxious about the advent of majority Labour government, Attlee was an effective solvent of anxieties.

A consensus favourable to a socialist programme required not the rejection of national identity but its redefinition. The hopes and the emotions of the 'People's War' appeared to offer some hope of this. Attlee's own sense of England was a regional one. He had celebrated this as a soldier in the bleakness of wartime Barrow in Furness. *I did not realise how much of a south countryman I was until my enforced exile. I loathe the north – the whole country is different from our kindly south and I find myself long for Devon and Somerset, Surrey and Sussex.*[7] His lifelong association with London did not diminish his political appeal. Although Morrison might be criticised as a parochial Londoner, Attlee, whose only significant time away from London was spent at university or in the army never was. His style, specific to class, time and geography, insulated him against such a limiting identification.

Attlee's rise to the leadership had parallels with that of his first Conservative counterpart, Stanley Baldwin. Attlee's survival in the 1931 election, when the rising stars of his generation tasted defeat, gave him an advantage that he never lost. Similarly Baldwin's route to the Tory leadership had been opened up by the Carlton Club meeting of October 1922, and the temporary but decisive marginalisation of more credible candidates. Both men benefited from a party reaction against flamboyant emotional and destructive leadership. Baldwin elevated second-class intellects above second-class characters. No one could ever claim of Attlee as was said of MacDonald – 'The platform is his confessional; the crowd his priest.'[8]

The security of Attlee depended upon his ability to establish a rapport with a trade union leadership suspicious of politicians' vanities and their potential for duplicity. His capacity to achieve this understanding fitted well with

Labour's authorised version of what had happened in 1931 and why. The party had to deal with the trauma of betrayal. If MacDonald and his cronies were to be cast as villains, the morality play required a hero. Arthur Henderson's political record was complex, but at critical moments he demonstrated an ability to position himself where the labour movement's centre of gravity appeared to be. This could be characterised as a high-minded devotion to the movement regardless of personal cost, or as a slavish pursuit of majority opinion. Either way such loyalty secured Henderson his place in Labour's pantheon. The seal of approval was Molly Hamilton's 1938 biography, an idealised portrait that was applauded by Attlee. In the final weeks of his own leadership Attlee could claim that *we haven't had a secretary we can trust since Arthur Henderson.*[9]

**What they said of Attlee:**

'We cannot have this man as our leader.' *Herbert Morrison in 1945.*

'A modest little man with plenty to be modest about.' *Attributed to Winston Churchill, more likely Claud Cockburn.*

'An empty taxi drew up in Downing Street and Clement Attlee got out.' *Unknown.*

'I love the little man.' *Ernest Bevin.*

'Precise, cold, correct – but with a certain dignity.' *Harold Macmillan in 1950.*

'His clipped, laconic sentences could dry up conversation within minutes.' *Barbara Castle.*

One strand in Henderson's mantle emphasised the significance of the trade union presence at the highest level of the party. Especially in August 1931 he had been the 'keeper of the cloth cap', the role taken by Ernest Bevin from 1945. But Attlee was also heir in his case to Henderson's fidelity as servant of the party. A sense of duty, a democratic ethos, albeit not always realised in practice – these became the approved party style. In the authorised version, Henderson, the loyal party servant had been used and then betrayed by the corruptible MacDonald. The Henderson ethos had to be represented at the top of the party. Attlee was a prime candidate.

Attlee's leadership involved dependence on colleagues to whom he gave significant autonomy in their own areas. He acted as facilitator and reconciler; at critical moments he could take the initiative. During his premiership this trait was particularly visible on international issues, most notably India, but also the Far East and Abadan. In contrast his grasp of economic problems was limited. Attlee effectively endorsed the views of economically-literate ministers as if these had the status of scientific opinion. Convertibility, devaluation, the 1951 rearmament programme – all posed basic challenges to the government. In these cases he did not act decisively. The 1947 crisis produced a threat to his own position and long-term electoral damage to his government. The rearmament controversy ended in divisive resignations.

Within their chosen area of reform Attlee and his ministers went much further than had seemed credible in 1939. The construction of a sizeable public sector and the fact and character of the National Health Service were abundant testimony to this. But in significant areas, the government attempted no reform. The pattern of post war education had been set by the 1944 Act. A product of Coalition compromise, this left intact the privileges of private education, whilst the state sector retained a system of selection damaging to working-class children. The Attlee government accepted this situation. The Prime Minister took pride in the Old Haileyburians within the Parliamentary Party. For him the evidence of the old school tie on the Labour benches was a demonstration of the party's inclusivity.

The government showed minimal interest in the reform of political institutions, reducing the delaying powers of the Lords and ending the university and business franchises. Ministers ignored issues of sexual equality. Such questions had been debated keenly before 1914, but had been displaced by a political agenda based on the economic and the social. Attlee's post-1918 prominence in Stepney had depended on the supercession of ethnic identities by ones based on class and occupation. From the 1920s Labour campaigned in the name of socialism for significant changes on a narrow front. From 1945 they implemented their programme as the first steps towards the creation of a socialist commonwealth.

What emerged was a social democratic modification of capitalism. This met long-standing demands for welfare, full employment and, for some, decent and affordable housing – in other words treatment as respectable citizens. Whether most Labour supporters wanted much beyond these essential priorities is debatable. The outcome, despite the austerity, was a decisive advance over most pre-war working class experiences. These achievements seemed secure. Maybe their realisation demonstrated that Labour's historical aims were achievable through a reformed capitalism. Yet much remained largely unchanged – institutions and culture, the distribution of wealth and power. The old order had been modified but had not disintegrated. That the coal owners had gone, but the public schools remained was perhaps an appropriate comment on the politics of Mr Attlee.

Attlee's self-characterisation as a Victorian suggested that his progressive politics were accompanied by a durable belief in Britain's continuing role as a major power. An Empire reformed gradually into a Commonwealth could be a benevolent influence in international affairs. Such aspirations could be expressed in the conventional categories of his generation. There was a need for harmony between *the white, the black, the brown and the yellow races*. The majority in South Africa were *primitive peoples. Natives* should be educated for self government.[10] As Prime Minister he had a strong awareness of Britain's economic and military weakness and was concerned to avoid sterile entanglements that would be costly in life and resources. A policy of judicious withdrawal proved compatible with a continuing British connection in India, Pakistan and Ceylon, but not in Burma. Such examples of necessity, disguised as principle, gave the government a reputation for enlightenment in imperial affairs. They depended on the effectiveness of administrative arrangement that would survive the British withdrawal. In contrast, the government's policy on Palestine ended in chaos and conflict. These episodes should not be read as early chapters in a decolonisation process that in two decades would liquidate the Empire. Attlee had little interest in Africa where British expectations of self-government were largely long-term. Immediate African priorities focused on economic development, both in agriculture and the production of valuable raw materials. The hope was that such an expansion of colonial production could both earn and save dollars. The needs of the British economy were the prime concern.

Questions of economic modernisation, institutional reform, ethnic rivalries and nationalism became entangled with the logic of the Cold War. In Malaya ministers reduced ethnic and economic complexities to a challenge by Communist and Chinese insurgents inspired, it was suggested, by Moscow. The Union of South Africa was regarded as a significant barrier against Communism. Labour ministers therefore allowed for the racial prejudices of the recently elected pro-apartheid government. Attlee underwrote such choices whilst remaining firmly committed to an expanding and multi-ethnic Commonwealth.

In contrast Ernest Bevin was the principal architect of the Anglo-American alliance. Initially Attlee's doubts about

Middle Eastern policy had suggested scepticism about any hostile dismissal of Soviet intentions. But he became thoroughly committed to American involvement in the defence of Western Europe, and to the accompanying denunciations of Communism. This commitment entailed a broader support for American policy even when, as in the Far East, this was assailed by reasonable doubts. Concerns were expressed over Korea and over American policy towards China, but in the end, except on the recognition of Communist China, there was acquiescence. For Attlee and for Bevin the relationship was largely free of illusions. The evidence of American self-interest and unpredictability was inescapable. This was far from an alliance of equals, but the maintenance of credibility as a great power necessitated American support. Bevin and his Foreign Office officials saw no alternative. By 1948 critics were dismissible as naïve idealists, or isolated as pro-Soviet apologists. The Cold War had two thoroughly negative consequences for the Attlee government. The burden of defence expenditure damaged the British economy, threatened the government's welfare achievements and precipitated the Cabinet split in the spring of 1951. More insidiously the Cold War corrupted the politics of the left. Complexities were reduced to dichotomies; arguments were displaced by crude ideological labels. Attlee and his colleagues insisted that democratic socialism offered the most effective response to Communism, but the space available for this politics had narrowed.

Such complexities militate against simple, perhaps celebratory, presentations of the Attlee years. One influential interpretation has characterised the Attlee achievement, not as distinctively socialist but as a second instalment in a progressive politics that was initiated by Edwardian Liberalism. This argument begins with the claim that the Attlee reforms, far from being the first steps in an advance to socialism, produced a more rational and more humane capitalism. There were obvious links with the welfare policies of the pre-1914 Liberal government. Moreover, two central intellectual influences on the Attlee government were Beveridge, briefly a Liberal MP, and Keynes, a star turn at the inter-war Liberal Summer School. Yet Attlee and his colleagues undeniably saw themselves as socialists. Self-identification and intention should be appreciated along with the consequences of policies. The Labour Party's ideological travails over the subsequent years of opposition become unintelligible without an appreciation of its continuing concern with socialism.

Attempted assimilation of the Attlee governments into such a progressive genealogy is often accompanied by the suggestion that the Labour Party was a flawed instrument of progress, compared with the potential, and some of the achievement, of Edwardian Liberalism. This characterisation rests typically on two propositions. The first concerns electoral viability. Attlee believed that a socialist appeal could be electorally successful. Only in 1945 was he decisively vindicated. Labour's electoral coalition depended for its durability on the political solidarity of specific, well-unionised working class occupations. The party found it hard to extend its appeal to other groups – manual workers with a less-established union commitment, white-collar workers, the southern English, the small towns and countryside. It took the geographic and social mobility of wartime to transcend these limitations. Such transcendence was often temporary.

This restrictive appeal is connected frequently to the second claim, the centrality of the trade unions both organisationally and culturally to Labour politics. Attlee's security as leader depended heavily on the trust extended to him not just by trade union leaders, but also by much of the unionised working class. Yet many erstwhile Liberals refused to give consistent support to such a party. Against this British experience stood an American counterpart. Roosevelt's New Deal coalition was broadly based and electorally powerful. The trade unions provided a significant but not a preponderant element. Arguably the frequent failure of so-called progressives to back Labour says more about their social stereotypes and antipathies than it does about the limitations of Attlee's party. Middle-class anxiety about working-class assertiveness, in other words self-confidence, raises serious doubts about any easy acceptance of claims about a post-war consensus. The record of the Attlee years does not suggest an administration dominated by the concerns of the trade unions. Consultation with union leaders was typically just that.

The relevance of these concerns to the politics of New Labour is obvious. The alleged progressive pedigree of the Attlee governments, and the suggestion that the union connection was a damaging constraint, may indicate a usable past that offers some legitimisation for Blair's policies. Such claims are poor history. Attlee and his colleagues were democratic socialists who positively endorsed the link with the unions. These characteristics might have been unattractive to some Liberals, but they did not prevent Attlee's governments from achieving more good for more people than any other British government of the 20th century.

This verdict can highlight Indian independence and the National Health Service. On the other side of the ledger stand the Cold War and the government's failure to significantly redistribute power and wealth. For some left-wing critics, the Attlee years were a lost opportunity to achieve a socialist breakthrough. This assessment emphasises the vigour of wartime and immediately post-war radicalism. Clearly there had been a popular shift to the left, but its extent and character remain unclear. In so far as it rested on admiration for the wartime Soviet Union, such radicalism eroded rapidly with the onset of the Cold War.

The claim of a lost opportunity also requires that ministers could have acted differently. Within narrow limits this was certainly the case. The imagination shown by Aneurin Bevan over the Health Service, or by Attlee and Cripps over India, was not a universal characteristic of the government. But a much more thorough reconstruction of society would have necessitated not the existing leadership acting differently, but a very different leadership. The Attlee generation had been formed by particular experiences of Labour and trade union politics. They also had deeply-rooted beliefs about the viability and fairness of existing institutions as instruments of reform. Wartime sacrifices, military victory and electoral success had strengthened this faith. Above all, the deepening Cold War blighted radical prospects, but to argue for a lost opportunity, is to claim that Britain's post-war international policy could have followed a radically different path. In the elections of 1950 and 1951 there was little evidence of a desire for policies significantly to the left of those followed by the government.

In retirement, Attlee remained extremely busy. He travelled by the Metropolitan Line to the Lords, lectured in the United States and reviewed books for the Sunday papers. An advocate of world government, he attacked any British attempt to join the European Common Market. When Vi Attlee died suddenly in the summer of 1964, he moved to a flat in the Temple. That October he campaigned in the general election for Harold Wilson's Labour Party. He revived the spirit of 1945, contrasting Tory concern for private profit with Labour's public spirit. Attlee the waspish schoolmaster made a cameo appearance. At the request of Labour's leadership, he reproved a senior Tory for an intemperate outburst.

*It is time he grew up. He ... acted like a school boy ... I hope that the Prime Minister will dissociate himself ... and administer an appropriate rebuke.*[11]

Attlee's world was vanishing. Churchill died in January 1965. At his funeral an increasingly frail Attlee was a pallbearer. The carefully choreographed ceremonial was a requiem to Empire. His own contribution made, Attlee the Victorian sat down exhausted on the steps outside Saint Paul's. For the last time Major Attlee had done his duty. Labour certainties disintegrated too. A decisive Labour election victory in March 1966 summoned up comparisons with Attlee's triumph. But in the face of economic difficulties, Wilson's electoral support collapsed. By-election defeats were spectacular demonstrations that the Labour solidarity of the Attlee years had vanished. In September 1967 Labour lost West Walthamstow, Attlee's last constituency, which had been held by Labour even in 1931. Seventeen days later, on 8 October, Attlee died. He had carefully made the funeral arrangements. The congregation sang William Blake's 'Jerusalem', evocative of his early days as a socialist. When his ashes were brought to Westminster Abbey, the hymns proclaimed his idealism and his patriotism – 'To Be a Pilgrim', and 'I Vow to Thee My Country'. His remains lie close to those of Ernest Bevin.

NOTES

## Chapter 1: An Unlikely Socialist

1 Attlee Papers 1/7. Churchill College Cambridge, hereafter Attlee Papers (C).

2. Attlee Papers (C) 1/7.

3. C R Attlee, *As It Happened* (Heinemann, London: 1954) p 13.

4. Cited in Kenneth Harris, *Attlee* (Weidenfeld & Nicolson, London: 1982) p 15.

5. Attlee Papers (C) 1/7.

6. Attlee Papers (C) 1/7.

7. Cited in Harris, *Attlee*, p 26.

8. C R Attlee to Tom Attlee, 2 April 1918. Attlee Papers Bodleian Library, Oxford, hereafter Attlee Papers (B).

## Chapter 2: Stepney and Parliament

1. Kenneth Young (ed), *The Diaries of Sir Robert Bruce Lockhart Vol 2 1939–65* (Macmillan, London: 1980) p 35, entry for 15 May 1940.

2. *Daily Herald*, 26 September 1921, cited in Harris, *Attlee*, p 53.

3. *New Leader*, 13 October 1922.

4. John Beckett, unpublished autobiography, Chapter 4.

5. Attlee, *As It Happened*, p 58.

6. House of Commons Debates Fifth Series Volume 159 col 93. 23 November 1922.

7. House of Commons Debates Fifth Series Volume 159 col 95. 23 November 1922.

8. Attlee Papers (C) 1/13.

9. Attlee Papers (C) 1/13.

10. C R Attlee to Tom Attlee, cited in Harris, *Attlee*, p 79.

11. *Daily Herald*, 19 July 1930.

12. C R Attlee to Tom Attlee, 1 November 1930. Attlee Papers (B).

13. C R Attlee to Tom Attlee, 23 August 1931. Attlee Papers (B).
14. Hugh Dalton, *Memoirs Call Back Yesterday* (Muller, London: 1953) pp 272–3.
15. Young (ed), *The Diaries of Sir Robert Bruce Lockhart Vol 1* (Macmillan, London: 1980), entry for 30 June 1932 at p 222.
16. C R Attlee to Ramsay MacDonald, no date, Ramsay MacDonald Papers. PRO 30/69 File 1315.
17. C R Attlee to Tom Attlee, 2 September 1931. Attlee Papers (B).
18. C R Attlee to Tom Attlee, 7 February 1933. Attlee Papers (B).
19. Labour Party Conference Report 1932, p 245.
20. C R Attlee to Tom Attlee, 18 October 1934. Attlee Papers (B).
21. C R Attlee to Tom Attlee, 3 April 1933. Attlee Papers (B).

## Chapter 3: Party Leader and War Cabinet Minister

1. Hugh Dalton, *Memoirs: The Fateful Years* (Muller, London: 1957) p 82; Norman and Jean MacKenzie (eds), *The Diary of Beatrice Webb Volume Four 1924–1943* (Virago, London: 1985), entry for 27 November 1935 at p 360.
2. C R Attlee to Tom Attlee 27 December 1937 Attlee Papers (B); statement on Spanish conflict cited in Harris, *Attlee*, p 139.
3. C R Attlee to Tom Attlee, 26 October 1936. Attlee Papers (B).
4. Cited in Harris, *Attlee*, p 136.
5. C R Attlee to Tom Attlee, 29 April 1938. Attlee Papers (B).
6. C R Attlee to Tom Attlee, 23 February 1939. Attlee Papers (B).
7. Cited in Harris, *Attlee*, p 177.
8. For this episode in January 1945 see Harris, *Attlee*, pp 241–5.
9. George Shepherd to George Ridley, 10 March 1943, cited in Stephen Brooke, *Labour and the War* (Oxford University Press, Oxford: 1992) p 310.
10. C R Attlee to Tom Attlee, 2 February 1943. Attlee Papers (B).
11. C R Attlee to Tom Attlee, 15 August 1944. Attlee Papers (B).
12. Attlee, *As It Happened*, p 148.
13. Dalton, *Memoirs: The Fateful Years*, p 482.

## Chapter 4: 'Annus Mirabilis'

1. *Let us Face the Future* (1945).

2. Attlee Papers (C) 1/17.
3. Francis Williams (ed), *A Prime Minister Remembers* (Heinemann, London: 1961) p 150.
4. Attlee Papers (C) 1/17.
5. Attlee Papers (C) 1/17.
6. Entry on Whiteley in *Dictionary of National Biography Supplement 1951–1960* (Oxford University Press, Oxford: 1971) pp 1048–9.
7. Attlee Papers (C) 1/17.
8. Attlee Papers (C) 1/17.
9. Attlee Papers (C) 1/17.
10. House of Commons Debates Fifth Series Volume 430 col 588, 18 November 1946.
11. House of Commons Debates Fifth Series Volume 430 col 580, 18 November 1946.
12. C R Attlee to Harold Laski, 4 June 1947, Laski Papers, University of Hull Library.
13. House of Commons Debates Fifth Series Volume 413 col 956, 24 August 1945.
14. Hugh Dalton, *Memoirs. High Tide and After* (Muller, London: 1962) pp 74–5.
15. Cab 195/3, Notes of Cabinet meeting, 6 November 1945.
16. Williams (ed), *A Prime Minister Remembers*, p 149.
17. C R Attlee to Tom Attlee, 12 August 1936. Attlee Papers (B).
18. C R Attlee, *The Labour Party in Perspective* (Gollancz, London: 1937) p 226.
19. David Dilks (ed), *The Diaries of Sir Alexander Cadogan OM* (Cassell, London: 1971) entry for 31 July 1945 at p 778.
20. Dilks (ed), *The Diaries of Sir Alexander Cadogan OM*, entry for 28 July 1945 at p 776.
21. House of Commons Debates Fifth Series Volume 430 cols 578–9, 18 November 1946.
22. Cited in Harris, *Attlee*, p 301. For background see Peter Weiler, *British Labour and the Cold War* (Stanford University Press, Stanford: 1988) p 108.
23. FO 800/476. Near Eastern Policy, 5 January 1947.
24. ME/47/4. Signed by Bevin.
25. *Let Us Face the Future* (1945).

26. Harris, *Attlee*, p 362.
27. House of Commons Debates Fifth Series Volume 420 col 1421, 15 March 1946.
28. As cited in Harris, Attlee, p 373. For the complexities see Peter Clarke, *The Cripps Version* (Allen Lane, London: 2002) pp 466–72.
29. Ernest Bevin to C R Attlee, 1 January 1947, FO 800/470.
30. C R Attlee to Ernest Bevin 2 January 1947, FO 800/470.
31. House of Commons Debates Fifth Series Volume 440 col 1227, 15 July 1947.
32. CM (47)76 20 September 1947, CAB 128/10.
33. PREM8/627/5 cited in Harris, *Attlee*, p 396.

## Chapter 5: 'Annus Horribilis'

1. George Brown, *In My Way* (Gollancz, London: 1971) pp 50–1.
2. *Daily Herald*, 24 February 1948 cited in Leo Panitch, *Social Democracy and Industrial Militancy. The Labour Party, the Trade Unions and Incomes Policy, 1945–1974* (Cambridge University Press, Cambridge: 1976) p 31.
3. C R Attlee to R S Cripps, 11 March 1950 cited in Peter Clarke, *The Cripps Version* (Allen Lane, London: 2002) pp 500–1.
4. House of Commons Debates Fifth Series Volume 446 cols 617 618, 23 January 1948.
5. *Daily Herald*, 3 May 1948, cited in Weiler, *British Labour and the Cold War*, p 277.
6. Cited in Harris, *Attlee*, p 422.
7. Philip M Williams (ed), *The Political Diary of Hugh Gaitskell 1945–1956* (Cape, London: 1983) p 137.
8. C R Attlee to Tom Attlee, 26 October 1949. Attlee Papers (B).
9. Cited in Harris, *Attlee*, p 439.
10. Sam Berger cited in Weiler, *British Labour and the Cold War*, p 229.
11. Attlee Papers (C) 1/17.
12. House of Commons Debates Fifth Series Volume 477 col 487, 5 July 1950.

13. Sir Oliver Franks to Kenneth Younger 23 July 1950 in *Foreign and Commonwealth Office Documents on British Policy Overseas* Series ii vol iv (HMSO: 1991) Doc 25 p 78, hereafter *FCO* Series ii vol iv.

14. Extract from Conclusions of Cabinet 29 November 1950 in *FCO* Series ii vol iv Doc 79 p 217.

15. Dean Acheson, *Present at the Creation* (Norton, New York: 1969: 1970) pp 478, 481.

16. See *FCO* Series ii vol iv Doc 116 pp 330–3 for Cabinet debate and for Gaitskell Williams (ed), *The Political Diary of Hugh Gaitskell*, pp 229–32.

17. For these Cabinet discussions on 26 January 1951, see *FCO* Series ii vol iv Doc 118 pp335–8.

18. See *FCO* Series ii vol iv Doc 121, dated 28 January 1951, pp 343–4

19. Williams (ed), *The Political Diary of Hugh Gaitskell*, p 216.

20. Williams (ed), *The Political Diary of Hugh Gaitskell*, p 245.

21. Williams (ed), *The Political Diary of Hugh Gaitskell*, p 246.

22. Shinwell on 23 May 1951, cited in William Roger Louis, *The British Empire in the Middle East 1945–1951* (Oxford University Press, Oxford: 1984) p 673.

23. Attlee on 14 May 1951, cited in Louis, *The British Empire in the Middle East*, p 662.

24. Cabinet minutes 12 July 1951, cited in Louis, *The British Empire in the Middle East*, p 669.

25. Cabinet minutes 27 September 1951, cited in Louis, *The British Empire in the Middle East*, p ???.

26. C R Attlee to Tom Attlee, 21 October 1951. Attlee Papers (B).

27. C R Attlee to Tom Attlee, 24 July 1951. Attlee Papers (B).

28. C R Attlee to Tom Attlee, 28 October 1952. Attlee Papers (B).

29. C R Attlee to Tom Attlee, 5 October 1952. Attlee Papers (B).

30. Williams (ed), *The Political Diary of Hugh Gaitskell*, p 383.

31. Janet Morgan (ed), *The Backbench Diaries of Richard Crossman* (Hamish Hamilton, London: 1981) entry for 27 September 1955, p 442.

## Chapter 6: Assessment

1. C R Attlee to Tom Attlee, 8 April 1954. Attlee Papers (B).
2. C R Attlee to Tom Attlee, 24 March 1957. Attlee Papers (B).
3. Cited in Harris, *Attlee*, p 560.
4. 'The Egoist' in *The New Statesman*, 24 April 1954.
5. Alan Bullock, *Ernest Bevin Foreign Secretary* (Heinemann, London: 1983) p 56. Bevin's use of this comparison is also indicated in the entry on Attlee by Maurice Shock in *Dictionary of National Biography Supplement 1961–1970* (Oxford University Press, Oxford: 1981) p 50.
6. Samuel H Beer, *Modern British Politics* (Faber, London: 1969) p 153.
7. C R Attlee to Tom Attlee, 20 March 1918. Attlee Papers (B).
8. Cited in Robert Skidelsky, *Politicians and the Slump. The Labour Government of 1929–1931* (Macmillan, London: 1967) p 65.
9. Morgan (ed), *Backbench Diaries of Richard Crossman*, entry for 27 September 1955 at p 442.
10. Attlee, *The Labour Party in Perspective*, Chapter IX.
11. Anthony Howard and Richard West *The Making of the Prime Minister* (Cape, London: 1965) pp 192–3. Attlee's target was Quintin Hogg, the issue the Profumo Affair.

CHRONOLOGY

| Year | Premiership |
|------|-------------|

*1945*  26 July: Clement Attlee becomes Prime Minister, aged 62.

Gandhi and Nehru reject British proposals and call on Britain to quit India

Nuremberg Trials open in Germany to judge crimes against peace, war crimes and crimes against humanity; the court rules that an individual's obedience to orders is not a defence.

*1946*  Feb: Naval mutinies in Bombay, Madras, Karachi and Calcutta.

Nationalisation of the Bank of England.

National Insurance Act, the Industrial Injuries Act and the National Health Act, founding the NHS, are all passed.

Trades Disputes Act repealed.

Coal industry nationalised.

USA drops atomic bombs on Hiroshima and Nagasaki. Japan surrenders to Allies.

Korea is placed under US and Soviet occupation, Outer Mongolia under Soviet control.

French refuse to recognise Ho Chi Minh's proclamation of the Democratic Republic of Vietnam.

. China, Nationalists under Chiang Kai-shek fight communists under Mao Zedong for control of Manchuria.

Arab League warns USA that creation of Jewish State in Palestine will lead to war.

United Nations charter is ratified by 29 nations.

Tito's National Front wins elections to Yugoslav constituent assembly.

Charles de Gaulle is elected president of France.

UNESCO is founded.

Karl Popper, *The Open Society and its Enemies.*

Benjamin Britten, *Peter Grimes.*

Richard Strauss, *Metamorphosen.*

Arts Council of Great Britain is established.

George Orwell, *Animal Farm.*

Jean-Paul Sartre, *The Age of Reason.*

Evelyn Waugh, *Brideshead Revisited.*

Films: *Brief Encounter. The Way to the Stars.*

---

UN General Assembly opens in London.

Yugoslavian constitution creates six constituent republics on the model of the USSR.

Juan Peron elected president of Argentina.

Churchill declares the Stalin has lowered an 'Iron Curtain' from Stettin to Trieste.

France recognises Vietnam as a democratic republic within the Indochinese Federation.

Truman signs bill of credit for $3.75 billion dollars for Britain.

Nuremberg establishes guilty verdicts for war crimes.

US Supreme Court rules that segregation on buses is unconstitutional.

Bertrand Russell, *History of Western Philosophy.*

Jean-Paul Sartre, *Existentialism and Humanism.*

Jacques Prevert, *Paroles.*

Eugene O'Neill, *The Iceman Cometh.*

Films: *Great Expectations. It's a Wonderful Life.*

Radio: Alistair Cook's *Letter from America* begins (series ends in 2004). *Woman's Hour. Dick Barton.*

| Year | Premiership |
|------|-------------|

1947    January: National Coal Board assumes control of the mines.
        February: Fuel crisis.
        July: Under the terms of the US loans agreement sterling is made
           convertible, prompting heavy selling in exchange for dollars.
        August: The government is forced to suspend convertibility of
           sterling. Official transfer of power in India: many killed in
           communal violence and six million people displaced.
        The Town and Country Planning Act is passed, making local
           councils produce plans for development.
        School leaving age raised to 15
        November: The UN General Assembly endorses the partition plan
           for Palestine.

1948    January: Nationalisation of the railways.
        Burma becomes an independent republic outside the
           Commonwealth.
        February: The White Paper on Wages and Personal Incomes, the
           first attempt by a post-war government at an incomes policy.
        The last British troops leave India.
        March: Members of the Communist Party are banned from working
           in the civil service or on work 'vital to the security of the state'.
        The Palestine Bill is passed by 242 votes to 32
        July: The Gas industry is nationalised.
        British Nationality Act
        The National Assistance Board is established.
        The Representation of the People Act abolished the business
           premises qualification to vote.

Hungary is reassigned its 1938 frontiers.

The Moscow Conference fails over the problem of Germany.

'Truman Doctrine' pledges to support 'free peoples resisting subjugation by armed minorities or outside pressures'.

US Secretary of State calls for relief aid to Europe.

Indonesian independence movement rises against Dutch troops, UN Security Council calls for ceasefire.

Communists win Hungarian election.

Italian government is centralised.

New Japanese constitution allows women to vote, limits the emperor's powers and renounces the use of war.

Edinburgh Festival is founded.

Albert Camus, *The Plague*.

Anne Frank, *The Diary of Anne Frank*.

Tennessee Williams, *A Streetcar Named Desire*.

Le Corbusier, Unité d'Habitation Marseille, France.

Films: *Monsieur Verdoux. Black Narcissus*.

---

Gandhi is assassinated in India.

Ceylon (Sri Lanka) becomes self-governing.

Czechoslovakia accepts an all-communist government.

Brussels Treaty is signed by Britain, France, Belgium, Netherlands, and Luxemburg for a 50-year alliance for military, economic and social cooperation.

Marshall Aid Act passed by Congress, contributing $5.3 billion to European recovery.

Israel is established and is recognised by USA and USSR.

South African Nationalists and the Afrikaner Party win election.

Yugoslavia is expelled from Cominform by USSR.

Berlin airlift is organised after USSR stops land traffic between West and Berlin.

Truman wins US Presidential Election.

Jackson Pollock, *Composition No.1*.

Columbia Record Company releases first LP.

Graham Greene, *The Heart of the Matter*.

Christopher Fry, *The Lady's not for Burning*.

Terrence Rattigan, *The Browning Version*.

Olympic Games held in London.

Film: *The Fallen Idol. Hamlet. Whisky Galore*.

Radio: *Take It From Here. Mrs Dale's Diary*.

Australian cricket team unbeaten on tour of England.

| Year | Premiership |
|------|-------------|

1949     April: North Atlantic Treaty Organisation (NATO) founded.
November: Iron and Steel Nationalisation Bill passed.
Republic of Ireland is proclaimed and leaves the Commonwealth.
India adopts constitution as a federal republic, remaining within the
    Commonwealth.

1950     North Korean forces invade South Korea; UN resolution demands
    their withdrawal and UN forces recapture Seoul then advance
    into North Korea.
NATO agrees to an integrated defence force under one commander.
Re-armament programme begins.
China enters Korean War and forces UN troops to retreat
    southwards; state of emergency is proclaimed in USA.
February: General election reduces Labour majority to five seats.

1951     North Korean and Chinese forces break UN line on 38th Parallel
    and take Seoul; UN troops defend at Imjin River.
Bevan and Wilson resign from Labour Cabinet over health service
    charges and defence expenditure.
26 October: Attlee leaves office after six years and 92 days.

| History | Culture |
|---|---|
| Chiang Kai-shek withdraws Nationalists to Formosa (Taiwan).<br>Statute of Council of Europe is signed in London.<br>Berlin blockade is lifted.<br>West Germany comes into being with its capital in Bonn.<br>Mao Zedong establishes People's Republic of China.<br>End of the Greek Civil War.<br>Legislation for apartheid begins in South Africa.<br>USSR tests its first atomic bomb. | Simone de Beauvoir, *The Second Sex*.<br>Gilbert Ryle, *The Concept of Mind*.<br>Jacob Epstein, *Lazarus*.<br>Rogers and Hammerstein, *South Pacific*.<br>George Orwell, *Nineteen Eighty-Four*.<br>Enid Blyton, *Little Noddy goes to Toyland*.<br>Arthur Miller, *Death of a Salesman*.<br>Films: *The Blue Lamp. Passport to Pimlico. The Third Man.*<br>US RCA produces colour television. |
| USSR and China sign 30-year Treaty of Friendship, France announces Schuman Plan for placing French and German coal, iron and steel under one authority which could be joined by others.<br>West Germany joins Council of Europe.<br>Alger Hiss is found guilty of concealing his Communist Party membership. | Moral and Pani, University City, Mexico.<br>Pablo Neruda, *General Song*.<br>Ezra Pound, *Seventy Cantos*.<br>Films: *Orphée. Rashomon. Sunset Boulevard.*<br>Radio: *The Archers. Listen with Mother.* |
| French elections cause ministerial crisis; Pleven forms coalition of the Centre.<br>Peace Treaty with Japan is signed by 49 powers, though not by USSR.<br>Peron is re-elected president of Argentina.<br>Chichekli leads Syrian coup.<br>Libya becomes independent federation.<br>Electric power is produced from atomic energy in USA. | Henry Moore, *Reclining Figure*.<br>Benjamin Britten, *Billy Budd*.<br>Stravinsky, *The Rake's Progress*.<br>Isaac Asimov, *Foundation*.<br>J D Salinger, *The Catcher in the Rye*.<br>Herman Wouk, *The Caine Mutiny*.<br>Jean-Paul Sartre, *Le Diable et le Bon Dieux*.<br>Films: *A Streetcar Named Desire. The African Queen. The Man in the White Suit.* |

# FURTHER READING

The entry on Attlee in *The Oxford Dictionary of National Biography* (Oxford University Press, Oxford: 2004) includes an extensive listing of sources for his correspondence. I have used material from the small collection at Churchill College, Cambridge, and drawn on the letters to his brother Tom in the more extensive, but still limited, collection at the Bodleian in Oxford. There is much material for his time in office at the National Archive in Kew, and letters can be found in the collections of several of his contemporaries.

Attlee's own writings offer illumination. *The Social Worker* (George Bell & Sons, London: 1920) contains insights into the development of his political ideas. *The Labour Party in Perspective* (Gollancz, London: 1937) is valuable not least because of his location of Labour socialism within an understanding of the distinctiveness of British political development. His subsequent attempts at autobiography, *As It Happened* (Heinemann, London: 1954), and the edited interviews with Francis Williams, *A Prime Minister Remembers* (Heinemann, London: 1961), are guarded. Some of the unpublished material in the Churchill College collection suggest the extent of this restraint.

Kenneth Harris's 1982 biography *Attlee* (Weidenfeld & Nicolson, London) benefits from the author's extensive conversations with the subject. It remains the dominant full-scale study, although perhaps stronger on personality than on politics. Trevor Burridge's 1985 work, *Clement Attlee. A Political Biography* (Cape, London), is detailed and provides a listing of Attlee's own writings. Amongst other biographers Francis Beckett's *Clem Attlee* (Politico's, London: 2000) presents a very empathetic portrait, whilst Roy Jenkins, *Mr Attlee. An Interim Biography* (Heinemann, London: 1948) is an early work by a backbencher whose father had been Attlee's Parliamentary Private Secretary. Attention should also be given to the detailed research by W Golant in 'The Emergence of C R Attlee as Leader of the Labour Party in 1935', *Historical Journal* (1970), and 'C R Attlee in the First and Second Labour Governments', *Parliamentary Affairs* (1973).

Short profiles of Attlee offer many insights . These include John Saville in *The Socialist Register 1983,* Kenneth Morgan in his *Labour People* (Oxford University Press, Oxford: 1987) and Peter Clarke in his *A Question of Leadership* (Hamish Hamilton, London: 1991). Maurice Cowling provides a perceptive portrait in his *The Impact of Hitler* (Cambridge University Press, Cambridge: 1975) at pp 388–91, Peter Hennessy, *The Prime Minister* (Allen Lane, London: 2000) epitomises the recent rise in Attlee's prime-ministerial reputation. The entries in the *Dictionary of National Biography*, the 1961–1970 supplement by Maurice Shock and the 2004 essay by Richard Whiting, each provide much information and give a strong sense of their subject. There is valuable material on Attlee's early years in Peggy Attlee, *With a Quiet Conscience. Thomas Simmons Attlee 1880–1960* (Privately published: 1995).

Understanding of Attlee is deepened by considering the careers of his colleagues, in some cases rivals. Ernest Bevin is presented powerfully and sympathetically over three volumes by Alan Bullock. The second volume (Heinemann, London: 1967), covers the wartime Coalition, the third (Heinemann, London: 1983) the Attlee governments. They can be complemented by the concise analysis by Peter Weiler published in 1993. Herbert Morrison is presented with care and understanding by Bernard Donoughue and George Jones in their

1973 study. There is significant material on the 1935 leadership election. Ben Pimlott's study of Hugh Dalton (Weidenfeld & Nicolson, London: 1985) was accompanied by two volumes of Dalton's extensive diary: together they reveal their subject in his complexity and help to explain Attlee's dominance over more flamboyant colleagues. Peter Clarke's *The Cripps Version* (Allen Lane, London: 2002) offers much on India, and significant insights on the 1930s and the period of Cripps' Chancellorship. Michael Foot's two-volume study of Aneurin Bevan (Mackibbon & Kee, London: 1962, 1973) is a passionate political statement that suggests a relatively modest assessment of Attlee as Prime Minister. The culture that shaped Bevan, and that Attlee perhaps failed to understand, is explored in Dai Smith *Aneurin Bevan and the World of South Wales* (University of Wales Press, Cardiff: 1993). The biographies of rising younger politicians give a good sense of life under Attlee; see for example, Philip Williams, *Hugh Gaitskell* (Cape, London: 1979) and Ben Pimlott, *Harold Wilson* (HarperCollins, London: 1992). *The Political Diary of Hugh Gaitskell* (Cape, London: 1983) edited by Philip Williams provides understanding of the actions of one of the protagonists in the crisis that was the Attlee Governments' finale. A diary giving illumination into an earlier difficult period in Attlee's leadership is Kevin Jefferys (ed), *Labour and the Wartime Coalition. From the Diary of James Chuter Ede 1941–1945* (The Historian's Press, London: 1987).

The Attlee government is thoroughly and sympathetically presented in Kenneth Morgan, *Labour in Power 1945–1951* (Oxford University Press, Oxford: 1984). A more sceptical assessment is Edward Thompson, 'Mr Attlee and the Gadarene Swine' in his *The Heavy Dancers* (Merlin Press, London: 1985). The basis for a tradition of radical criticism of the Attlee governments can be found in Ralph Miliband,

*Parliamentary Socialism* (Merlin Press, London: 1961). A contrasting position which has its own critical stance on the politics of labourism is David Marquand, *The Progressive Dilemma* (Heinemann, London: 1991). Peter Hennessy, *Never Again. Britain 1945–1951* (Cape, London: 1992) is an accessible reconstruction of the Attlee years. Any assessment of the Attlee years requires an analysis of the politics of the Churchill Coalition. Paul Addison, *The Road to 1945* (Cape, London: 1975) is a seminal and controversial study. Stephen Brooke, *Labour and the War* (Oxford University Press, Oxford: 1992) illuminates the complexities of Labour responses to the opportunities and difficulties of the Coalition.

Economic policymaking by the Attlee governments is analysed in Alec Cairncross, *Years of Recovery* (Methuen, London: 1985). Richard Toye carefully examines the character of and limits to Labour's commitment to planning in *The Labour Party and the Planned Economy 1931–1951* (The Boydell Press, Woodbridge: 2003). The first chapter of Leo Panitch, *Social Democracy and Industrial Militancy* (Cambridge University Press, Cambridge: 1975) analyses the development of a wages policy after 1945. The creation of the National Health Service and the events leading to the crisis of 1951 are meticulously presented in Charles Webster, *The Health Service Vol 1 Problems of Health Care. The National Health Service Before 1957* (HMSO, London: 1988). The problems posed for the government by the politics of consumption are assessed in Ina Zweiniger-Bargielowska *Austerity in Britain. Rationing, Controls and Consumption* (Oxford University Press, Oxford: 2000). This should be complemented by James Hinton, 'Militant Housewives: the British Housewives' League and the Attlee Government', *History Workshop Journal* (1994).

The view of foreign policy in Bullock's study of Bevin can be contrasted with John Saville, *The Politics of Continu-*

*ity. British Foreign Policy and the Labour Government 1945–46* (Verso, London: 1993) and Peter Weiler, *British Labour and the Cold War* (Stanford University Press, Stanford: 1988). Attlee's differences with Bevin over the Middle East are discussed in Saville, Chapter 5, and in R Smith and J Zametica, 'The Cold Warrior: Clement Attlee Reconsidered, 1945–7', *International Affairs* (Autumn 1988) pp 631–47. The decision to construct a British atomic bomb is presented in Margaret Gowing, *Independence and Deterence: Britain and Atomic Energy Vol 1 Policymaking* (Macmillan, London: 1974).

The complexities of the Government's response to the Indian crisis can be appreciated in R J Moore, *Escape From Empire : the Attlee government and the Indian problem* (Oxford University Press, Oxford: 1983). Palestine, Abadan and much else are presented with authority and clarity in William Roger Louis, *The British Empire in The Middle East 1945–1951* (Oxford University Press, Oxford: 1984). Valuable context for Palestine is provided in Michael J Cohen, *Palestine and the Great Powers 1945–48* (Princeton University Press, Princeton: 1982 )

Understanding of Attlee's security within the post-war Labour Party requires an appreciation of its internal distribution of power. Robert McKenzie, *British Political Parties* (Heinemann, London: 1955) is a classic work that took as enduring what proved to be contestable. Samuel H Beer, *Modern British Politics* (Faber, London: 1965) combines the analysis of the distribution of power in political parties with an appreciation of the significance of ideas. Martin Harrison, *Trade Unions and the Labour Party since 1945* (Allen & Unwin, London: 1960) offers scholarship in an area notable for exaggeration and myth.

# Picture Sources

Pages 6–7
Herbert Morrison and Clement Attlee photographed during the Socialist Party Conference in Margate, 3 October 1950. (Courtesy Topham Picturepoint)

Page 124
Clement Attlee and King George VI in the grounds of Buckingham Palace on VJ Day, 15 August 1945. (Courtesy Topham Picturepoint)

Page 144–5
Clement Attlee and his wife Violet leave Downing Street at the beginning of a 1,000-mile election tour, 8 February 1950. (Courtesy Getty Images)

# Index